The Diamond Cutter Sutra

Publisher's Acknowledgment

The publisher gratefully acknowledges the generous help of the Hershey Family Foundation in sponsoring the production of this book.

The Diamond Cutter Sutra

A COMMENTARY BY

Dzogchen Master Khenpo Sodargye

Wisdom Publications
199 Elm Street
Somerville, MA 02144 USA
wisdomexperience.org

Library of Congress Cataloging-in-Publication Data
Names: Suodaji, Kanbu, 1962– author.
Title: The Diamond cutter sutra: a commentary /
    by Dzogchen Master Khenpo Sodargye.
Description: Somerville, MA: Wisdom Publications, [2020] | Includes index.
Identifiers: LCCN 2020001541 (print) | LCCN 2020001542 (ebook) |
    ISBN 9781614295860 (paperback) | ISBN 9781614296096 (ebook)
Subjects: LCSH: Tripiṭaka. Sūtrapiṭaka. Prajñāpāramitā. Vajracchedikā.
Classification: LCC BQ1997 .S86 2020 (print) | LCC BQ1997 (ebook) |
    DDC 294.3/85—dc23
LC record available at https://lccn.loc.gov/2020001541
LC ebook record available at https://lccn.loc.gov/2020001542

ISBN 978-1-61429-586-0   ebook ISBN 978-1-61429-609-6

24 23 22 21 20
5 4 3 2 1

Translated by Ke Jiang. Line drawing of Manjushri on cover by Andy Weber. Cover and interior design by Gopa & Ted2, Inc.

Printed on acid-free paper that meets the guidelines for permanence and durability of the Production Guidelines for Book Longevity of the Council on Library Resources.

Printed in the United States of America.

Please visit fscus.org.

Contents

Preface

Many people fail to understand that all their sufferings
come from various attachments.
How to dispel this attachment?
The Buddhadharma offers the most supreme pith instructions
and skillful means for this.
With the Buddhadharma,
even though attachment remains,
it is possible to get over difficulties more easily without going to
    extremes.
Then the sky becomes more open and vast.

THE WISDOM THAT CUTS DIAMONDS

THE LIFE OF every individual is full of changes and fluctuations of
happiness, anger, sorrow, and joy. All these seem truly existent, but if
you study the *Diamond Cutter Sutra*, you will realize that this is not the true
essence of life. Life's essence lies only in cutting the attachment toward all
phenomena and realizing that there has never been anything such as an "I."

Attachment is the only root cause of all our suffering. Even if our attachment is as small as the tip of a needle, it can still cause us unending distress.
No matter what you are attached to, once you get it, you are afraid of losing
it; once you do lose it, your heart is broken. If there were no attachment,
then what suffering would you have?

Whether Buddhist or not, many people like to say they are "giving up
attachment" and that they have come to think that "all phenomena are
emptiness, so there is no need to attach to vice or virtue." Since they are
unable to discern what to adopt and what to abandon, they behave unscrupulously. Ironically, when they fall into this trap, they end up with the
worst attachment, the horrendous attachment to emptiness. The Buddha
taught this seemingly paradoxical truth: "It is better to have attachment as

gigantic as Mount Meru to 'existence' than attachment as tiny as a mustard seed to 'nonexistence.'"

So how do we destroy attachment appropriately, without being led astray? The *Diamond Cutter Sutra* explains that although at the ultimate level nothing exists, and even the concepts of "vice" and "virtue" are indeed just another attachment, nevertheless, at the conventional level all phenomena still appear, and in that dream-like, illusory reality, the law of cause and effect is inerrant. So if we do not want to suffer at the relative level, we have to give up vice and adopt virtue.

Before recognizing the nature of mind, we must hold on to things that are virtuous and right. Like a boat, they can help us cross a river, so until we reach the other shore it makes no sense to give them up. Otherwise, if we throw away the boat in the middle of the river, what is going to happen? The answer is obvious.

Even if you do not understand the meaning of this sutra, its blessings and benefits are there. When hardship, illness, or misfortune befall you, just transcribing or chanting this sutra once can help immensely. Merely keeping a copy of this sutra in your house or carrying one around with you can pacify all sorts of calamities and bring immense auspiciousness, just like a Buddha stupa.

By all accounts, the merit of the *Diamond Cutter Sutra* is inconceivable. People who are fortunate enough to see it, hear it, or touch it will swiftly cut off the root of suffering and reach the other shore of everlasting peace and happiness. It works for everyone, no matter whether you believe in Buddhism or not!

Sodargye
Larung Gar, Sertar

Introduction

Homage to Buddha Shakyamuni!
Homage to the wisdom warrior, Manjushri!
Homage to the kind lineage masters!

The subtlest, most profound, and unsurpassable sublime Dharma
can be encountered only once in hundreds and thousands of kalpas.
Since I am fortunate enough to be able to listen to it and uphold it
    today,
may I understand the original meaning of the Tathagata.

In order to liberate all sentient beings, may we generate the unsurpassable
supreme bodhicitta!

THE *DIAMOND CUTTER SUTRA* CAN PACIFY DISASTERS

THE *Diamond Cutter Sutra*, also called the *Three Hundred Verses of Prajna: The Transcendental Wisdom*, has enormous influence in Chinese-dominated regions. Every Chinese Buddhist school, whether Chan, Huayan, or Pure Land, has placed great importance on this particular sutra. It has also been included in many people's daily chanting practice. Since its first translation into Chinese by the great translator Kumarajiva around 402, numerous practitioners have clearly recognized the nature of mind and countless people have avoided calamities by its blessings.

Moreover, unlike other prajna doctrines, it also occupies a pivotal position in Tibetan Buddhism. In Tibetan areas it is a common practice to recite the *Diamond Cutter Sutra* one hundred times and the *Liberation Sutra* one thousand times within the first forty-nine days after a person has died, in order to ensure this person's liberation. People also often recite the *Diamond Cutter Sutra* in long-life prayer ceremonies. Many versions of this sutra scribed in gold and silver have been found at the Jokhang in Lhasa and in the ancient book collections of Inner Mongolia. Understanding its meaning is thus very relevant.

In the past there was an alarming trend among some people who studied Tibetan Buddhism. When they returned to their homes in the Chinese areas, they started to belittle or disrespect the *Diamond Cutter Sutra*, possibly because after studying Tibetan Buddhism, especially Vajrayana, they realize the nature of mind is not merely emptiness but the union of luminosity and emptiness, which view is held higher than the Middle Way. Through this book, I seek to deliver one message: Tibetan Buddhism and Chinese Buddhism do not contradict each other but are perfectly integrated in one taste. Since the excellence of the *Diamond Cutter Sutra* is inconceivable, spread its wisdom whenever there is the opportunity. This will bring immense benefit for both self and others.

Some people asked me to teach this sutra from the view of the Great Perfection, others asked me to explain it from the view of Mahamudra. However, my personal intention is to explain this sutra so that people will understand its actual meaning; if you have not yet understood its meaning from the view of Sutrayana, or Middle Way, it is unrealistic to jump to the unsurpassed tantric instructions. Therefore, let us first clear up the meaning from the view of Sutrayana. Once we master the ultimate view of the Middle school expounded in this sutra, it will be much easier to reach an understanding from the view of the Great Perfection and Mahamudra.

EVEN THE TRANSLATIONS OF THE *DIAMOND CUTTER SUTRA* ARE HIGHLY BLESSED

Several translations of the *Diamond Cutter Sutra* have existed in Chinese areas, the earliest of which was translated by Kumarajiva (343–413) in the Later Qin of the Dong Jin dynasty (317–420). Afterward, this sutra was also translated by Bodhiruci (ca. fifth to sixth century) during the Northern Wei dynasty (386–534), Paramartha (499–569) during the Southern dynasty, Dharmagupta during the Sui dynasty (581–618), and Xuan Zang (602–664) and Yi Jing (635–713) of the Tang dynasty.

Among all the translations, Yi Jing's version is closest to the Tibetan version, while Kumarajiva's version differs somewhat from it. There are several possible reasons for these discrepancies. At the time of Kumarajiva, Buddhism was still flourishing in India, and so there might have been different Sanskrit versions. Furthermore, since Kumarajiva's translation assembly had over five hundred people, there was a greater chance of some mistakes slipping into the transcription of his interpretation. Nevertheless, as his translation was blessed by the truthful speech of great accomplishers, chanting it can create inconceivable merit. This has been proven by the countless numbers of people who have attained enlightenment by relying on this version.

As for the Tibetan *Diamond Cutter Sutra*, there is only one existing translation. After comparing the various versions from Lhasa, Qing Hai, and so forth, I found they are all exactly the same as the version found in the Prajna (Perfection of Wisdom) section of the Kangyur, the standard canon of the Buddha's teachings.

For this teaching I use Kumarajiva's translation, along with the translations by Xuan Zang and Yi Jing for reference, since Yi Jing's is closest to the Tibetan version. My modern English translation of the sutra passage, bolded and italicized, is perfectly faithful to the original sutra as translated by Kumarajiva into ancient Chinese. After the translation comes my commentary on the sutra passage. My commentary occasionally refers to Xuan Zang's and Yi Jing's versions or to the Tibetan edition in order to give the contemporary reader the deepest perspective possible on the sutra passage.

THE STRUCTURE OF THE TEXT

Usually sutras are not divided or structured according to an outline. If you have not yet studied any sutra, keep in mind that they often have repetitions that may sometimes obscure the meaning. Commentaries, however, have chapters and sections based on an outline whose intent is usually to clarify ambiguities and highlight relevant passages from other sutras.

Even though it is said to be just a translation of the sutra, Kumarajiva's version adds some features of a commentary in that it has been divided into thirty-two chapters. This division does indeed make it easier for readers to understand the meaning stage-by-stage. This arrangement is not found in the Tibetan version or other Chinese translations. It is almost certain that this thirty-two-chapter arrangement was added not by Kumarajiva but by Crown Prince Zhaoming of the Liang dynasty. Some people may say, "No conceptual thoughts should ever be added in sutras; therefore, since he divided the sutra into chapters, Crown Prince Zhaoming has been suffering in the hells until now." We cannot be certain that this is true, however.

Generally speaking, no conceptual thoughts should be added to the sutras, as they are the words of the Buddha. If the intention is not to slander the text, however, adding chapters or outlines to help readers understand cannot be of great fault. Since ordinary people are unable to judge the correlation of a karmic cause and its effect, I am unable to find out whether it is indeed the worst offense that Crown Prince Zhaoming put his own ideas in the arrangement of Kumarajiva's *Diamond Cutter Sutra*.

It happened once that a lay practitioner, based on his own interpretation, mixed *Finding Comfort and Ease in the Nature of Mind on the Great Perfection* and *The Guide of Three Topics and Three Virtues* together, which resulted in something completely incoherent. So I wrote a letter to tell him that we ordinary beings are not qualified to mix teachings in this way and asked him to quit altering the vajra words of the omniscient Longchenpa. Following this logic, Crown Prince Zhaoming's arrangement is indeed inappropriate. Nonetheless, what he did does help us to understand the meaning of this sutra, and so, according to the Chinese Buddhist tradition, we will study this sutra in thirty-two chapters.

According to Tibetan Buddhism, the way to teach a sutra is to divide it into three parts: the Initial Virtue—the Title, the Middle Virtue—the Meaning, and the Virtuous Ending—the Conclusion. I will also follow this convention. Now, let us study these one by one.

The Initial Virtue—The Title

Why the Simile "Diamond" for This Sutra?

Diamond/Vajra

Why call it a "diamond" sutra? In the *Sadhana of Destroying Demons*, a diamond, or vajra, is said to have seven attributes: it is indestructible, unbreakable, unchangeable, and so forth. According to Buddhist accounts, the diamond held by Indra is indestructible and yet able to destroy a mountain. Thus the unique attribute of a diamond is that it can destroy everything but not be destroyed by anything. Similarly, the emptiness of prajna[1] can destroy all wrong views but not be destroyed by any kind of wrong view. Hence the term "diamond," or "vajra," as a simile.

Prajnaparamita

Prajnaparamita is a Sanskrit word meaning "transcendental wisdom reaching the other shore," or the "perfection of transcendental wisdom." The beginning of the Tibetan version of the sutra says, "Homage to All Buddhas and Bodhisattvas." The forty-first Tibetan king, Tritsuk Detsen Ralpacan, declared that all sutras begin like this in order to demonstrate that a given text, in this case the *Diamond Cutter Sutra*, falls in the basket of the collection of sutras in the Tripitaka, or Buddhist canon.

In the Tibetan version and some Sanskrit versions, the complete title of this sutra is *Vajra Cutter: Perfection of Wisdom Sutra* (Sanskrit: *Vajracchedika Prajnaparamita Sutra*). Among the Chinese versions, Xuan Zang's and Yi Jing's translations kept the same complete title.

The Middle Virtue—The Meaning

1. The Cause of This Teaching

Thus have I heard, once the Bhagavan was dwelling in Shravasti, at the Jeta grove of the Anatapindada garden, together with a great sangha of 1,250 monks.

THE FIVE PERFECTIONS OF THE TEACHINGS BY THE BUDDHA

"ONCE WHEN Buddha Shakyamuni was living with a sangha of 1,250 fully ordained monks at Jetavana Anatapindada garden in Shravasti, I heard the Buddha say thus." According to Mahayana, this passage explains the five perfections:

1. The perfect place: Jetavana Anatapindada garden in Shravasti.
2. The perfect time: sometime after Buddha Shakyamuni reached buddhahood.
3. The perfect followers: 1,250 fully ordained monks.
4. The perfect teaching: the profound meaning explained in the *Diamond Cutter Sutra.*
5. The perfect teacher: the guide of the three realms, Buddha Shakyamuni.

Thus have I heard, once
These words, added by sutra compilers, mean, "I heard these vajra words at that time." What did they hear? The *Diamond Cutter Sutra* that is about to be explained.

Before entering the great parinirvana, Buddha Shakyamuni gave permission to Ananda and other disciples to compile the three baskets (Tripitaka) of teachings: the Sutra, Vinaya, and Shastra. In order to demonstrate the authority of a sutra, they should add (1) at the beginning, "Thus have I heard, once"; (2) connections in the middle, like "the Bhagavan asked" and

"Manjushri answered"; and (3) at the end praise, like "gods, nagas, humans, asuras, and gandhavas all rejoiced."

Furthermore, sutras fall into three categories: taught by the Buddha in person, taught through the blessings of the Buddha, and taught with the permission of the Buddha. "Thus have I heard" was not said by the Buddha in person but it was added with permission of the Buddha.

After the Buddha entered parinirvana, three councils were convened to compile the Buddha's doctrines. There is disagreement on when these councils were held. Some say they occurred two years after the Buddha's parinirvana, others say 110 years, or 180 years, or close to 400 years after. It is impossible to be certain. What is known is that through these three compilations, the Tripitaka was written down.

In regard to the compilation of the Tripitaka, it is generally agreed that the Sutra Pitaka, or Basket of Discourses, was compiled by Ananda, who was the foremost disciple in scholarship and memory; the Vinaya Pitaka by Upali, who was the foremost disciple in upholding pure precepts; and the Abhidharma Pitaka by Mahakasyapa, the disciple who was unexcelled in ascetic practices.

Since the *Diamond Cutter Sutra* belongs to the Sutra Pitaka, "I" in "Thus have I heard" refers to Venerable Ananda.

"Once" could be explained in two ways:

1. When the Buddha gave a teaching. There have been debates on how long the Buddha taught the Dharma. Some believe for forty-nine years, while others say for only forty-five years. Since it was not clearly recorded in which year and on which day this *Diamond Cutter Sutra* was taught, here "once" could be explained as one day.

2. When an ordinary being gives a Dharma teaching, it must have a specific time, place, audience, and subject, but for the Buddha, these are not necessarily fixed. The Buddha could give various teachings to different sentient beings in countless worlds in the past, in the present, and in the future simultaneously. This state is inconceivable and unfathomable. In this way, "once" could also include the three times of past, present, and future.

Shravasti

According to the *Commentary on the Ornament of Clear Realization*, just like Vaishali and Sarnath, Shravasti was one of the six great cities of ancient India and was ruled by King Prasenajit at the time of the Buddha.

Jetavana Anatapindada garden

There is a story about this garden: After taking refuge in the Buddha, the lay practitioner Anatapindada requested the Buddha to give teachings in Shravasti and planned to buy land to build a monastery there for the Buddha. He searched and found that the garden of Prince Jeta was pleasant, peaceful, and suitable for meditation. So he explained to the prince his intention to buy this land.

Reluctant to sell this garden, the prince joked with him, "Unless you can cover the whole land with gold, I will not sell it." Since he had made offerings to six buddhas in his past lives, Anatapindada had the supreme merit of being able to see treasures buried underground. So he went home, opened his treasure house, and with the help of his elephants, transported enough gold to cover the land.

Inspired by his earnestness, Prince Jeta said, "When we discussed this transaction, we didn't include the trees. The land is now yours, but the trees are still mine. Let's offer this garden to the Buddha together."

Afterward, this garden was named the Jetavana Anatapindada garden. As promised, Anatapindada erected an assembly hall, and the Buddha often taught the Dharma there.

When visiting India in 1990 with my lama, Jigme Phuntsok Rinpoche, we went on a pilgrimage to this famous Jetavana Anatapindada garden. However, we saw only ruins and rubble; no monastery and no city remain.

It is chronicled that Buddha Shakyamuni displayed clairvoyance and subjugated the six masters of the heretics at that site. In memory of this event, each year Lhasa holds ceremonious Dharma gatherings from the first to the fifteenth day of the month of miracles, the first month in the Tibetan calendar, and our Buddhist institute also holds a fifteen-day Dharma Gathering of Vidyadharas.

Together with a great sangha of 1,250 monks [bhikshus]

In the Tibetan version and Yi Jing's Chinese translation, besides the 1,250 fully ordained monks, it says there were also "great bodhisattvas" in attendance. In my view, their translations were based on one Sanskrit version. Kumarajiva's and Xuan Zang's translations, which are slightly different, do not mention "great bodhisattvas." I believe this is because they used different Sanskrit versions.[2]

As we know, it is very common to see discrepancies in the phrasing and even the contents of Indian scriptures, so when encountering different translations, avoid asserting "this is authentic, that is fake." Never simply agree on one version and be against another. Instead, understand that all these sutras were compiled by panditas with the dharani of never forgetting. Since their capacity for never forgetting varied, understand how very common it is to see inconsistencies among different translations.

For our discussion here, we will follow the view that, among the Buddha's audience, besides monks of the Basic Vehicle, the Theravada, there were also bodhisattvas of the Great Vehicle, the Mahayana. Therefore this sutra belongs also to the Mahayana.

WHY INFERIOR FOOD TURNS INTO AMBROSIA IN THE BUDDHA'S MOUTH

Then, when it was time to eat, the Bhagavan put on his robe, held his bowl, and entered the great city of Shravasti to request food.

Put on his robe

If the Bhagavan had to straighten his robes before going out, there is no need to mention why we followers need to do the same. As disciples of the Buddha, make whatever you wear look pleasing. Certainly this is not to encourage you to spend lots of time dressing and grooming yourself, but rather to encourage you to dress and behave in a manner that ordinary people do not get the wrong view, thinking that Buddhists are weird.

After Dharma study, some people think they have seen through everything, so they become sloppy and go about unkempt and unwashed. They believe this is a necessary "high state" for a Buddhist, but in fact they have just gone to extremes. The result is that their family members start to worry but keep quiet in order to avoid conflict, and their colleagues remain at a respectful distance from them. Actually, proper dress and a decent appearance are essential for lay practitioners and are also a skillful means for benefiting sentient beings.

Request food

Some people might question, "Why does the Buddha become hungry at lunchtime like us and have to go out requesting food?" As a matter of fact, it was to help sentient beings accumulate merit and to give Dharma teachings that the Buddha went out to request food, and not because of his own hunger.

The *Sutra on the Inconceivable Secret* says, "Like a gold ball, the Buddha's body has no innards." The *Golden Light Sutra* also says, "It appeared that Buddha Shakyamuni was requesting food, but he never needed the food because the Buddha could never be hungry." Even if Buddha Shakyamuni was hungry, he could simply turn earth, wood, and rocks into food through his power of clairvoyance, and so he would have no need to beg for food. Through his power of blessing, one item becomes many and insipid food becomes ambrosial. As said in the *Ornament of Clear Realization*: "In the mouth of the Buddha, even inferior food can turn into nectar."

During a three-month rain retreat in Veranja, Buddha Shakyamuni and his disciples suffered a famine due to crop failures. The Buddha was afraid that Ananda would not be able to stand such great hardship, since he was of royal birth, so he gave him a grain of wheat. After eating it, Ananda had no hunger for seven days. Ananda was amazed and gained enormous faith in the blessing of the Buddha. Moreover, the Buddha had the samadhi of Akasagarbha, which could gather all worldly wealth. Therefore there is no real need for the Buddha to request food.

Some people say, "Buddha Shakyamuni is the king of beggars." This is obvious slander and has immense demerit. Although the Buddha did lead bhikshus to beg for food in the city, this was simply a manifestation. Likewise, even though the Buddha had uprooted his attachment toward "I," he still appeared to say "my disciple" and "my patrons."

IT IS OF FOREMOST IMPORTANCE TO KEEP THE BODY STRAIGHT UP WHILE MEDITATING

In the city, after begging for food door to door, the Buddha returned. After having his meal, he put away his robe and bowl, washed his feet, and sat on his throne.

Begging

This is still a common practice in Thailand. Holding bowls and walking barefoot, monks are usually on the streets before daybreak. Donors come out even earlier and wait with food in their hands at intersections, then joyfully line up and make offerings to the monks once they see them coming. Besides food, they also offer personal hygiene items and clothes. Monks usually have very large bowls and always come back with full bowls. After having breakfast, they have enough left for lunch.

In India, begging time is usually sometime before noon. However, as said in the sutras, on a few occasions monks go to beg at noontime. How-ever, this does not happen in Thailand.

Washed his feet

Washing the feet after eating a meal is also a tradition in Thailand. In the past, when Geshe Sherab Gyatso visited Thailand, the king himself served the water for him to wash his feet. When we visited Thailand, we didn't have such preferential treatment, but some lay practitioners did serve us water for washing our feet.

Sat on his throne

After washing his feet, the Buddha sat straight up on his Dharma throne. It is important to keep our body straight while teaching or listening to the Dharma and when meditating. Some people like to lean back while reading books and chanting prayers; this is very bad. If our body is not straight, the channels are not straight, and this greatly affects our mem-ory and meditation. Tibetan Buddhism always emphasizes body posture; whether chanting prayers or meditating, our body must be straight and sitting cross-legged.

We can understand that the Buddha had his meal, washed his feet, per-haps relaxed on his cushion for a while, resting in mindfulness, and then was ready to teach the *Diamond Cutter Sutra*.

2. Subhuti Asks Questions

HERE IS THE PROPER WAY TO PAY HOMAGE TO BUDDHAS AND BODHISATTVAS

At that time, in the assembly, the Elder, Subhuti, rose from his seat, bared his right shoulder, knelt down on the ground with his right knee, folded his palms together, and respectfully asked the Buddha:

IN XUAN ZANG'S translation, prior to this it has: "Then, a great number of monks arrived where the Buddha was. After prostrating at Bhagavan's feet, circumambulating him clockwise three times, they walked backward and sat on one side." This means that after the Buddha finished his meal and sat straight up, the 1,250 fully ordained monks and great bodhisattvas came to the Buddha, prostrated at the Buddha's feet with reverence, circumambulated him clockwise three times, and then backed away to one side and sat down.

Paying homage

Paying homage has three forms: superior, middling, and inferior. The superior form is the homage of realization, the middling is the homage of practice, and the inferior is to pay homage respectfully through the three doors with the five body parts touching the earth. Here, it seems to refer to the ordinary homage with the three doors.

How exactly did they pay homage? Each disciple, one after the other, came to the Buddha, knelt down with reverence, and gently touched the crown of their head to the feet of the Buddha. According to Gendun Chophel, this manner of homage was adopted from the royal court of ancient India. In order to show their respect, subordinates and ministers would touch the crown of their heads to the feet of the king, who sat on a high throne. Similarly, in order to show their reverence, Buddhist disciples followed the same manner to prostrate to the Bhagavan. In the *Kalachakra* of the Vajrayana, when a guru gives empowerment, disciples must some-times also pay homage like this.

Circumambulating him clockwise three times [in Xuan Zang's version]
Generally speaking, counterclockwise circumambulation creates the demerit of destruction, while clockwise circumambulation has the merit of construction. Tibetan people are so afraid of destroying merit that they are terrified at the sight of someone circumambulating counterclockwise.

Once when I was visiting Mount Wutai, I saw some people circumam-bulating the Great White Stupa counterclockwise. An old lama traveling with us was so distressed that he blocked their path to prevent them from continuing, but since he did not speak any Chinese, he had to show them with his body and hand gestures.

The Buddha explained the merit of circumambulating clockwise in the *Sutra on the Merit of the Clockwise Circumambulation of Stupas.*

Subhuti
Subhuti is the questioner and the key figure in the *Diamond Cutter Sutra*. Though he appeared as a monk of the Basic Vehicle, he was in fact emanated by Bodhisattva Manjushri. His name is often present in sutras on prajna, or transcendental wisdom. Having completely mastered the intended mean-ing of prajna, he was the first person allowed to give teachings on prajna after the Bhagavan finished his discourses on the Great Vehicle.

Bared his right shoulder
He had his robe over his left shoulder and bared his right shoulder.

Knelt down on the ground with his right knee
Generally speaking, when praying in front of one's guru, the disciple puts the left foot and right knee on the earth. This is a proper posture.

WHO CAN BRING HAPPINESS TO US IN PRESENT AND FUTURE LIVES?

"How wondrous! Bhagavan, the Tathagata, has taken good care of all the bodhi-sattvas and has counseled all the bodhisattvas."

How wondrous! Bhagavan

In this world, countless great religious leaders and spiritual teachers have failed to bring genuine liberation to sentient beings, but Buddha Shakyamuni managed to do so. Here, Subhuti cannot help himself from praising and acclaiming how wondrous it is!

Tathagata

Tathagata is one of the ten honorific titles of the Buddha. Based on his various excellent qualities, the Buddha was given the epithets of Tathagata, Arhat, the Correctly and Fully Awakened One, the One Perfect in Knowledge and Conduct, Sugata, the Knower of the World, the Supreme Trainer of Men to Be Subdued, the Teacher of Gods and Humans, the Buddha, and Bhagavan. The detailed qualities for each title have been expounded by Mipham Rinpoche in his *Commentary on the Sutra of Recollecting the Three Jewels*.

All the bodhisattvas

In the Tibetan version, it says "bodhisattva mahasattvas," which means the great bodhisattvas. Some scriptures define "bodhisattvas" as those who are on the first to seventh stages, or bhumis, and "great bodhisattvas" as those on the eighth to tenth stages. Here this term is consistent with the definition in Shantideva's *Guide to the Bodhisattva's Way of Life*—anyone who has given rise to bodhichitta deserves the epithet "great bodhisattva."

Has taken good care of

"Has taken good care of" is in Kumarajiva's translation, while Yi Jing translates this as "benefited," and Xuan Zang has "accepted." In comparison, Yi Jing's translation is closer to the Tibetan version, but all three translations basically have the same meaning.

What is the most supreme care? It is to bestow true happiness and benefit on sentient beings in the present and for future lives. It would not be the most supreme if it were with wealth and fame that we were taken care of. So how is this care bestowed? It is the Buddha's guidance that leads us away from the suffering of cyclic existence and brings us true happiness in present and future lives.

Has counseled
The Indian Buddhist scholar Kamalashila said that the Tathagata has enjoined sentient beings to practice three kinds of reliances: to rely on a qualified teacher wholeheartedly, to rely on the authentic Dharma for one's practice, and to rely on the supreme instructions to benefit sentient beings.

DARE TO ASK THE BUDDHA WHERE TO SETTLE THE MIND

"Bhagavan, how should a son or daughter of noble qualities who has given rise to the perfect, unsurpassable bodhichitta abide? How to subjugate the mind?"

The Tibetan version and the translations of Yi Jing and Xuan Zang also includes the words "how to abide, how to practice, and how to subdue the mind," which seems not to be included in Kumarajiva's translation. It might be missing in the Sanskrit version he used or perhaps it slipped in translation. Both are possibilities.

The question raised by Subhuti contains all the contents of the ground, the path, and the fruition of the Great Vehicle. The ground is how to abide after generating bodhichitta. The path is how to practice the six perfections and ten thousand actions. The fruition is how to train the mind to attain buddhahood. From my point of view, his question could be explained either as the ground, the path, and the fruition or simply as a question to introduce the ensuing content.

After Subhuti asked these three questions, Buddha Shakyamuni started to answer.

EACH AND EVERY SINGLE CHARACTER IN A SUTRA HAS EXTREMELY PROFOUND MEANING

The Buddha said, "Good, good, O Subhuti. It is exactly as you have said: the Tathagata has taken good care of all the bodhisattvas and has well counseled all the bodhisattvas. Listen attentively as I explain to you in what way a son or daughter of good qualities who has given rise to the perfect, unsurpassable bodhichitta must settle and subjugate the mind."

"Thus shall I do, Bhagavan. I would love to listen to you with joy."

At first glance, this part of the sutra seems repetitive, but if you scrutinize the passage carefully, you will find it is not redundant at all. It was to acknowledge Subhuti's questions and show that he understood them that the Buddha rephrased them in this way.

Suppose someone said, "Khenpo, it is marvelous that you taught us the *Diamond Cutter Sutra*. How wondrous the teaching is! How should we practice it afterward?" I might reply, "So it is, so it is. It is indeed marvelous that I taught you the *Diamond Cutter Sutra*. In regard to how to practice it afterward, listen carefully, I am going to tell you now . . ." In order to show that the teacher has listened well and understands the student, the question is traditionally repeated more than once, and in that way the attention of the audience is kept on the teaching.

Good, good

Subhuti was in this way commended by Buddha Shakyamuni. When delighted by what their disciples have done, gurus usually utter praise such as, "Good, good!" "Right, right!" "Thus it is, thus it is."

Right after this commendation, the translations of Xuan Zang and Yi Jing have: "Listen attentively, retain it firmly in your heart, as I am going to expound to you in proper order how great bodhisattvas subjugate the mind." This means, "O Subhuti, you should listen carefully, engrave these [words] in your heart, and never forget them. Let me explain to you step-by-step."

Listen attentively

Sutras are different from other texts; each word and every sentence have profound meaning. Many great masters like to stress this before giving a Dharma teaching: "Listen attentively and give up chatting, otherwise I cannot give you this teaching. Even Buddha Shakyamuni demanded this. If you cannot concentrate, there will be no benefit for you."

Subjugate the mind

It is not enough to just listen. One must retain the meaning of the teaching in one's mind, learn it by heart, and never forget it.

The *Diamond Cutter Sutra* mainly focuses on how to eliminate attachment and subjugate one's mind. From the view of the Indian Buddhist master Kamalashila, the entire sutra can be summarized in three sections: (1) how to give rise to bodhichitta at the beginning, (2) how to practice the six paramitas (perfections) in the middle, and (3) how to train one's mind and attain the state of the inseparable rupakaya (form body) and dharmakaya (truth body) in the end.

3. The Genuine Great Vehicle

HOW TO GENERATE BODHICHITTA

The Buddha told Subhuti, "This is how great bodhisattvas subjugate their mind: for all the sentient beings of different classifications—born from eggs, from wombs, from moisture, spontaneously, with form, without form, with perception, without perception, with neither perception nor nonperception—I will liberate them all to enter nonabiding nirvana. Even though numerous, countless, and limitless sentient beings are liberated in this way, ultimately there is no sentient being that is liberated."

THE FIRST SENTENCE describes conventional bodhichitta, the second one explains ultimate bodhichitta. Specifically, in order to liberate all sentient beings as infinite as space in number, I make the aspiration to attain unsurpassable enlightenment. This is conventional bodhichitta. Ultimate bodhicitta can be understood through the three spheres that are empty of true essence: actor, receiver, and action. The bodhisattvas who are able to liberate beings do not inherently exist, the sentient beings who are to be liberated do not exist, and the action of liberation does not exist either.

Keep in mind that to liberate all sentient beings is a bodhisattva's greatest responsibility in this world; without such bodhichitta, any virtuous root would not increase. But in the end we must understand that in the ultimate meaning there is no sentient being to be liberated.

THE NINE CLASSIFICATIONS OF BEINGS

In the three realms of cyclic existence, there are numerous sentient beings who vary greatly. Generally speaking, there are nine classifications of beings: born from eggs, from wombs, from moisture, spontaneously, with form, without form, with perception, without perception, and with nei-ther perception nor nonperception.

1. Born from eggs

This category of sentient beings includes nagas, birds, and a few humans—for example, I have heard one story of a sailor merchant, who while at sea lived with a crane; they had two children, named Dza and Newadza, who hatched from eggs.

In a Tibetan folktale, King Gesar was said to be born from an egg. As the legend goes, one very snowy day, his mother, who was working as a maid, did not go to work, as she was about to give birth. In a rage that she did not show up for work, the master rushed to her house with a knife in his hand. After entering her house, he saw his maid sleeping deeply. Furious, he pulled the comforter off. To his surprise, there was a giant egg in her bed. Undeterred by his surprise, he hacked at the egg. The egg cracked and three babies appeared. One flew to the sky; the second, King Gesar, fell on the tent because his knee was hit by the knife; and the third, Shampa, was thrown into a river by the angry master. However, no historical records support the authenticity of this legend.

2. From wombs

Human beings and a great number of animals are born from wombs. According to the *Treasury of Abhidharma*, most often hungry ghosts are also born from wombs.

3. From moisture

In the summer most insects are born from moisture. At the time of the Buddha, it was not unheard of for a human being to be born in such a way. The lady born from a mango tree in the *Nirvana Sutra* is such an example. As far as we know, it does not happen these days.

4. Spontaneously

Gods, demigods (*asuras*), human beings at the beginning of this kalpa, and hell beings are all born spontaneously. Moreover, some great accom-plishers, such as Guru Padmasambhava and Aryadeva, were also born spontaneously.

5. With form

This refers to sentient beings in the desire realm and form realm. In the *Treasury of Abhidharma*, it is explained that due to clinging to the five sensory enjoyments, sentient beings in the desire realm have extremely gross attachment, and so have physical bodies. In contrast, beings born in the form realm have eliminated the gross clinging found in the desire realm, and so they do not have carnal bodies, but since they still have subtle attachment, they have luminous bodies. Since beings in both realms have form, they are called "beings born with form."

6. Without form

"Without form" indicates sentient beings born in the formless realm. They do not have a tangible form but only the form of consciousness. Since such form is extremely subtle, they are called "beings born without form."

7. With perception

This points to one type of god that lives in the Great Fruition Heaven of the fourth dhyana heaven. In this abode, beings are free from the gross conceptual thoughts of those in the desire realm, but they still have subtle conceptual thoughts.

8. Without perception

This corresponds to some gods that abide around the perimeter of the Great Fruition Heaven. In the *Commentary of the Treasury of Abhidharma*, the Great Fruition Heaven is compared to a city, and this abode at the perimeter is likened to monasteries outside the city. Gods born here have conceptual thoughts only twice: at birth and at death. Other than that, they have no single thought for five hundred great kalpas.

9. With neither perception nor nonperception

This is called the "Peak of Existence," the heaven with neither perception nor nonperception, or the highest heaven of the formless realm. Lacking the conceptual thoughts found in the form realm or desire realm, it is without perception; since there is still extremely subtle and extremely unobvious consciousness, it is without nonperception. As the *Treasury of Abhidharma* says, this abode does not lack consciousness. There are still conceptual thoughts clinging to meditative concentration, but since they are extremely subtle, it is described as without perception.

WHAT IS CONVENTIONAL BODHICHITTA?

All sentient beings in cyclic existence fall within one of these nine categories. Bodhisattvas of the Great Vehicle aspire to liberate them by helping them to dissolve their contaminated bodies and conceptual thoughts into the basic space (dharmadhatu) and thereby attain non-abiding nirvana. This is conventional bodhichitta.

As the *Ornament of Clear Realization* says, "In order to benefit sentient beings, I generate bodhichitta and pursue the perfect, unsurpassable enlightenment."

WHAT IS ULTIMATE BODHICHITTA?

Although numerous, countless, and limitless sentient beings are liberated in this way, ultimately there is no sentient being that is liberated.

Strictly speaking, only when such understanding arises can one become a bodhisattva in the real sense. As said in *The Introduction to the Middle Way*, "Hereafter, since such a mind has risen, he or she alone shall be called a 'bodhisattva.'"

If conventional bodhichitta and ultimate bodhichitta are in union, then, as it is said in the *Avatamsaka Sutra*, "wisdom is the reason for not dwelling in the three realms; compassion is the reason for not abiding in nirvana." From the perspective of conventional bodhichitta, it is out of great compassion that bodhisattvas do not forsake sentient beings; from the perspective of ultimate bodhichitta, it is because of the wisdom of emptiness that bodhisattvas do not fall into cyclic existence.

SUBHUTI'S QUESTIONS ON THE TWO KINDS OF BODHICHITTA

Earlier, Subhuti brought up three questions: how to abide, how to practice, and how to tame one's mind. Through the above analysis, this can be answered at both the conventional and ultimate levels, respectively:

Conventional bodhichitta. Abide by giving rise to conventional bodhichitta. Practice by liberating sentient beings, whose numbers are as infinite as the limitless sky. Tame one's mind by generating bodhichitta at all times and places.

Ultimate bodhichitta. Abide with no sentient being to be liberated and no one to liberate them. Practice while abiding in such a state. Tame one's mind by dissolving conceptual thoughts of clinging to the intrinsic existence of all phenomena into dharmadhatu.

WHAT IS A TRUE BODHISATTVA?

Why is it that bodhisattvas liberate sentient beings at the conventional level, but no sentient beings are liberated at the ultimate level?

"Why is that? Subhuti, if a bodhisattva has the idea of the characteristic of a self, the characteristic of a person, the characteristic of a sentient being, and the characteristic of a living being, this bodhisattva is not a bodhisattva in the real sense."

Regarding the ultimate truth, it is a terrible mistake to think of liberating or helping sentient beings. Anyone who grasps characteristics, thinking, "I will liberate them and bring them to supreme nirvana" is actually not a bodhisattva but an ordinary person. Why? At the ultimate level, all characteristics are unfindable: the bodhisattva who has generated bodhichitta does not exist intrinsically, the sentient beings who will be liberated do not exist intrinsically, and the bodhichitta that arises is also as unsubstantial as dreams and illusions. Actually, this is the highest state of the great perfection. It would be fascinating to interpret the meaning of the *Diamond Cutter Sutra* with Longchenpa's *Finding Comfort and Ease in Illusion on the Great Perfection.*

Characteristic
Xuan Zang translated this as "perception." Here, "characteristic" and "perception" have the same meaning. Both denote grasping with conceptual thoughts and are closely related to conceptual thoughts. In Chinese, the terms "characteristic" (相) and "perception" (想) are sometime used in ancient texts interchangeably; the term "perception" (想) is made up of the term "characteristic" (相) on top of the term "mind" (心).

The Tibetan version does not include "the characteristic of a self" but does include the other three characteristics.

The characteristic of a self

The characteristic of a self is that its existence relies on the same single continuum.

The characteristic of a person

The characteristic of persons is that they live in the contaminated world with the defiled body aggregates.

The characteristic of a sentient being

The characteristic of sentient beings is that they take rebirth in cyclic existence in one of the three realms based on their karma and afflictive emotions.

The characteristic of a living being

The characteristic of living beings is that they have one continuous life span from the same fully ripened effect. For instance, some people desperately fear death and wish to live as long as a hundred years. This is the characteristic of a living being.

To believe that these four characteristics intrinsically exist is a great obstacle on the path to liberation. With these four characteristics implanted in the mind, nobody can reach genuine liberation. Therefore Je Tsongkhapa said, "Once the attachment toward characteristics is eliminated, the view is consummated at that very moment."

From the very beginning to the end, the *Diamond Cutter Sutra* talks about eliminating attachment toward intrinsic existence.

4. The Wonderful Practice without Fixation

LEARN HOW TO PRACTICE GENEROSITY FROM BODHISATTVAS

HAVING UNDERSTOOD the problem of the four characteristics, we now go further to understand that bodhisattvas should not fixate on anything or have any attachment to any intrinsic existence of perspective, view, practice, conduct, or fruition.

"Moreover, Subhuti, bodhisattvas should practice generosity without fixating on any phenomenon. That is, to practice generosity without fixating on form, to practice generosity without fixating on sound, smell, taste, touch, and dharma."

A genuine bodhisattva does not attach to the intrinsic existence of anything. Here the Buddha takes the example of generosity in the six perfections: when bodhisattvas practice generosity, they have no attachment to the six sense objects, which are form, sound, smell, taste, touch, and dharma.

Form
Ordinary people have attachment toward the color, shape, and appearance of the beggar. For instance, they discern the appearance of a beggar dressed in shabby clothes to be bad and so forth. However, having realized emptiness, bodhisattvas are free from attachment to the intrinsic existence of any form.

Sound
When a beggar comes to the house and says, "Please have a heart and give me something," a bodhisattva, upon hearing this voice, does not conceive the thought, "All right, let me give you something right away!"

Smell
The nose of a bodhisattva does not discern whether something has a pleasant or unpleasant smell.

Taste
Bodhisattvas do not judge whether something tastes delicious or disgusting and do not make choices accordingly.

Touch
Through body contact, bodhisattvas do not distinguish whether something is heavy or light, hard or soft, rough or smooth, and so forth.

Dharma
Dharma is the object of consciousness. Not having the conceptual thoughts to grasp any dharma, bodhisattvas do not think, "I gave ten dollars to a beggar, it must create immense merit."

Many Tibetan monasteries recite a prayer composed by Bodhisattva Maitreya. One line goes, "not fixating on any dharma, practice generosity with no miserliness." *The Introduction to the Middle Way* also says, "Since the giver, the recipient, and the gift are all empty, generosity is named 'transcendental perfection.'" The giver, the receiver, and the gift are in the nature of great emptiness. If we practice generosity by abiding in such a state, it is genuine and it is the ultimate perfection of generosity.

Here generosity is just one example. We practice the other five perfections—discipline, patience, diligence, meditative concentration, and wisdom—in the same way.

Earlier, Subhuti asked how to abide, how to practice, and how to tame one's mind. Here the answer is given again: to abide in the emptiness of the three spheres, to practice the six perfections with the emptiness of the three spheres, and to tame one's mind by eliminating attachment to intrinsic existence.

THE MERIT WOULD BE IMMEASURABLE WHEN GIVING IN THIS WAY

"Subhuti, bodhisattvas should practice generosity without fixating on any characteristics. Why is that? If bodhisattvas practice generosity without fixating on any characteristics, the merit is inconceivable."

What is the ultimate generosity? It is generosity imbued with the emptiness of the three spheres—that is, a giving that is empty of self, other, and object.

Generally speaking, when practicing generosity, ordinary people have attachment toward the three spheres, whereas bodhisattvas do not. Since they have no attachment at all, the merit they attain is immeasurable. By accumulating merit through this mode of generosity, it is easy to achieve the perfect, unsurpassable buddhahood.

Certainly we have not yet realized the emptiness of the three spheres, but many lamas have taught that if, while practicing generosity, we at least recall this aspiration, "However buddhas and bodhisattvas of the past practiced generosity, may I too practice generosity in the same way now," we can gain almost equal merit.

"Generosity" Is Like Dreams and Illusions

The following sutra passage employs the metaphor of space to explain this inconceivable merit further:

"Subhuti, what do you think? Is the space to the east conceivable?"
"No, Bhagavan."
"Subhuti, is the space to the south, the west, the north, and the four intercardinal directions as well as above and below conceivable?"
"No, Bhagavan."
"Subhuti, similarly, if bodhisattvas practice generosity without fixating on any characteristic, their merit is also inconceivable. Subhuti, bodhisattvas should follow this instruction in any case."

While practicing generosity, Buddhist practitioners of the Great Vehicle visualize the emptiness of the three spheres to the greatest extent possible. Although impossible for ordinary people, if one comprehends that conventionally, generosity is like a dream and an illusion, and that ultimately all phenomena are of great emptiness and are free from all mental fabrications, this understanding is quite close to the emptiness of the three spheres.

People who have not yet been exposed to the view of the Middle Way are extremely concerned about the impact of their even minuscule generosity. However, as anyone who has studied the Middle Way must know, conventionally, the action of giving to a beggar is good, but ultimately, I do not exist, the beggar does not exist, and the gift in this action does not exist, so it makes no sense to aggrandize it and hold on to something nonexistent.

Some people, though they have literally understood this, are still quite unwilling to practice generosity. For instance, when they are having a meal in a restaurant and a beggar approaches, instead of grasping this good opportunity, they feel quite uncomfortable giving anything to the beggar. To avoid embarrassing themselves, they give a little bit, involuntarily. This is neither the emptiness of the three spheres nor genuine generosity!

5. The True Meeting

WHAT IS THE TRUE FACE OF THE TATHAGATA?

EARLIER, the Buddha told Subhuti that in practicing generosity abiding in the emptiness of the three spheres, the merit would be immeasurable. This statement has been connected to the following root text by this question: Through practicing generosity, one can accumulate merit for now, and then in the future attain the excellent qualities of the form body (rupakaya) of the Buddha with the thirty-two major marks and the eighty minor marks, but do these excellent marks exist intrinsically?

"Subhuti, what do you think? Can the Tathagata be met through body marks?"

"No, Bhagavan, the Tathagata cannot be met through body marks. Why? The body marks described by the Tathagata are not body marks."

The Buddha told Subhuti, "All the characteristics are delusive. Only by seeing that characteristics are not characteristics can the Tathagata be truly met."

The Buddha told Subhuti, "Characteristics all arise from delusive conceptual thoughts. Only when we understand that all characteristics lack intrinsic existence can we meet the true Tathagata."

Buddha Shakyamuni has a golden body, a protuberance (*ushnisha*) on the crown of his head, and marks of the Dharma wheel on the soles of his feet. Does it mean that when seeing a body with these marks, one has met a Tathagata?

If we were not Subhuti, it is very possible we would answer, "Yes, yes, of course." However, Subhuti had studied very well, so he shook his head and said that conventionally, the Tathagata manifested a variety of excellent marks before sentient beings so that he could guide numerous sentient beings onto the path of liberation, but when examined with the approaches to ultimate analysis, these are not the true body marks of the Tathagata.

It would be wonderful if disciples could comprehend his intended meaning. After hearing the answer, the Buddha was delighted and affirmed that whether good or bad, in samsara or nirvana, anything that has characteristics is delusive, false, and totally contrived by conceptual thoughts. Only when we have realized that all characteristics are not characteristics can we meet the true Tathagata.

6. The Rarity of True Faith

IT IS FORTUNATE TO GAIN FAITH IN THE *DIAMOND CUTTER SUTRA*

Subhuti said to the Buddha, "Bhagavan, when some sentient beings in the future hear the words and explanations of this sutra, will they gain true faith?"

The Buddha told Subhuti, "Quit saying this. In the last five hundred years of the Dharma-degeneration age after the Tathagata passes away, there would be people upholding precepts and accumulating merit. They would gain faith in the words of this sutra and hold it to be truthful. You should be aware that these people have practiced virtuous roots before, not only one, two, three, four, or five buddhas but thousands and hundreds . . . even numerous buddhas before. If hearing the words of this sutra gives rise to one thought of pure faith, Subhuti, the Tathagata can completely know and perceive that these sentient beings will gain infinite merit."

The last five hundred years of the Dharma-degeneration age

THE LAST five hundred years of the Dharma-degeneration age has been explained in two ways: (1) It refers to the current Dharma-degeneration age of the five degenerations. "Five hundred" is not necessarily the specific number but simply signals a long time. (2) According to Kamalashila's view, Buddha Shakyamuni's teaching would remain in this world for 2,500 years. On average, each 500 years is a particular phase. There are five phases in total and "the last 500 years" refers to the last phase.

Over 2,500 years have passed since the time of the Buddha. Does this mean our advanced years are not counted as a phase of the Buddha's teaching according to Kamalashila's calculation? The answer is no. In Tibet all the lineages and schools have acknowledged that the teachings of the Buddha would remain for 5,000 years. The Phurba school, with Patrul

Rinpoche and Mipham Rinpoche as its main figures, believes that we are now in the period after 2,900 years, while the Sakya school believes that it has been over 3,000 years since the start of this buddha age. Nevertheless, the teachings of the Buddha will remain for about another 2,000 years.

The astrological calculation of the Phurba school is known to be precise. Using *The Wheel of Time*, they calculate the occurrence of solar and lunar eclipses accurately to the minute and second. In their calculation of the time frame of the Buddha's teachings, they referred to specific celestial phenomena. For instance, Venus (called the "Daybreaking Star" by the ancient Chinese) appeared in the sky while the Buddha attained enlightenment, and a solar eclipse occurred on the next day, so they concluded it has been over 2,900 years since the time of the Buddha.

People upholding precepts and accumulating merit
This is how Kumarajiva's translation refers to those who uphold pure discipline, accumulate merit, and have wisdom. Xuan Zang translated the same passage as "[people] with shila, with good qualities, and with wisdom," while Yi Jing translated it as "with precepts, with good qualities, and with wisdom."

These people have practiced virtuous roots before . . . thousands and hundreds . . . even numerous buddhas before
This is the reason for encountering the *Diamond Cutter Sutra*. The secret tantra also says that implanting virtuous roots before countless buddhas in our past lives is the reason for encountering the Great Perfection in this life. The omniscient Longchenpa said in the *Treasury of the Supreme Vehicle*, "Anyone who has encountered the unsurpassable Vajrayana must have made offerings to countless buddhas and have been among the entourage of Buddha Samantabhadra."

If hearing the words of this sutra gives rise to one thought of pure faith
Buddha Shakyamuni told Subhuti that in the future, if sentient beings give rise to a thought of pure faith in the *Diamond Cutter Sutra*, they can accumulate infinite merit.

Since we are fortunate enough to listen to the *Diamond Cutter Sutra*, we should rejoice in our own merit and cultivate faith in the view of emptiness. The merit of the view of prajnaparamita is inconceivable. Even reasonable doubt regarding emptiness—for example, thinking, "Is it possible that all phenomena lack inherent essence?"—could destroy the root of cyclic existence. As said in *The Four Hundred Stanzas on the Middle Way*, "People with little fortune would not think to even doubt this Dharma,[3] but those who even slightly doubt it can destroy the three realms."

Can completely know

Through his wisdom, the Buddha knows absolutely that in the future numerous sentient beings will gain faith in the *Diamond Cutter Sutra*, and he knows unerringly their capacity and their causes and so forth. For instance, now that we are studying the *Diamond Cutter Sutra*, the Buddha Shakyamuni knows precisely and unerringly the answers to questions such as: What kind of faith have we gained in the sutra's meaning? What are the causes that would allow each individual to gain such faith? What kind of merit have we accumulated before countless buddhas?

Perceive

Even scenes of future sentient beings listening to and reflecting on the *Diamond Cutter Sutra* would be vividly perceived by the Buddha through his wisdom eyes. For instance, Buddha Shakyamuni can clearly see that we are sitting in this packed assembly hall and that a couple of people are dozing off surreptitiously.

These sentient beings will gain infinite merit

Since we have accumulated merit before numerous buddhas and have gained faith in the *Diamond Cutter Sutra*, the merit is so vast that no space can contain it.

WITH THE VIEW OF EMPTINESS, LIBERATION CAN BE SWIFTLY FULFILLED

"Why is that? These sentient beings do not grasp the characteristic of a self, the characteristic of a person, the characteristic of a sentient being, and the characteristic of a living being; neither do they grasp the characteristic of dharma nor the characteristic of non-dharma."

The four characteristics were explained earlier, but Kamalashila has interpreted them differently. Unlike the previous definitions, which are more from the perspective of the object, this interpretation is more from the perspective of the subject, so in this case we can substitute the term "characteristic" with the term "conception."[4]

The characteristic of a self: grasping the composition of the five aggregates—form (the physical world), sensation (our basic responses to experience), perception (interpretation of sense objects by mental labeling), mental formations (triggered by some object, which produce karma), and consciousness (including thoughts)—as a self.

The characteristic of a person: the clinging to the idea of "mine," derived from ego-clinging.

The characteristic of a sentient being: grasping taking rebirth as a human in this life, a god in the next life, a being in lower realms in future lives; sentient beings have ceaselessly taken rebirth in cyclic existence.

The characteristic of a living being: grasping the life of a mindstream that continues without interruption.

Once one has gained faith in the meaning of emptiness in the *Diamond Cutter Sutra*, one can transcend the four conceptions in a short time, and people with sharp faculties can even reach liberation right away. Just as a fish that has been hooked will immediately leave the water, once we gain the view of emptiness, though our physical body does not transform much and still appears as an ordinary being, yet in the near future we will definitely leave the ocean of cyclic existence for the other shore of liberation.

Since "the characteristic of dharma" and "the characteristic of non-dharma" will be expounded in following text, let's skip them for now.

In fact, once we realize the emptiness of one phenomenon, we are able to realize the emptiness of all phenomena. That is why once we understand the meaning of emptiness in the *Diamond Cutter Sutra*, we are able to understand the meaning of emptiness of all phenomena. *The Four Hundred Stanzas on the Middle Way* also says, "The emptiness of one phenomenon is indeed the emptiness of all phenomena." Therefore we can see the benefit of studying the *Diamond Cutter Sutra*.

What Hinders Us Is Not the Appearance of Phenomena but Our Attachment to Them

The appearance of phenomena does not hinder us, but our attachment to phenomena does; when we grasp at them, what are the disadvantages? The disadvantages have been analyzed in three ways: (1) the disadvantage of grasping characteristics, (2) the disadvantage of grasping on to existent dharma, and (3) the disadvantage of grasping on to non-dharma.

1. The Disadvantage of Grasping Characteristics

"Why is that? If sentient beings hold on to a notion of 'characteristics,' they would grasp a self, a person, a sentient being, and a living being."

Any grasping toward characteristics is an obstacle on the path to enlightenment. Venerable Tilopa said, "What hinders us is not the appearance of phenomena but our attachment to them."

When our mind does not hold on to the notion of "characteristics," we transcend all phenomena; but once the notion of "characteristics" occurs, we grasp the four characteristics. Although a self, a person, a sentient being, and a living being represent different aspects of the same characteristic, their essence is the same.

Grasping at Phenomena Is the Root Cause of Cyclic Existence

2. The Disadvantage of Grasping on to Existent Dharma

"Once holding on to a notion of the characteristics of dharma, we grasp a self, a person, a sentient being, and a living being."

The characteristics of dharma

The characteristics of dharma covers not only the Buddhadharma that pacifies all afflictive emotions but also existent phenomena that appear within the conventional view. Grasping on to any of the characteristics of phenomena will result in the above-mentioned four conceptions that prevent us from reaching the ultimate buddhahood. The *One Hundred Thousand*

Verses on Prajnaparamita says, "Subhuti, even if grasping on to name and characteristic is as miniscule as the tip of a hair, authentic buddhahood cannot be attained."

Clinging to existent phenomena within the conventional view is grasping the five aggregates, which in turn leads to the grasping of a self (the characteristic of a self), the grasping of what belongs to this self (the characteristic of a person), the continuous rebirth of a sentient being (the characteristic of a sentient being), and the longevity of this living being in cyclic existence (the characteristic of a living being). With these four conceptions, sentient beings would inevitably create karma, enter cyclic existence, and suffer endless birth and death. *The Precious Garland of the Middle Way* says:

> Whenever there is grasping on to the five aggregates,
> there would be grasping to a self,
> which in turn results in karma,
> and karma again leads to existence.

GRASPING AT EMPTINESS IS INCURABLE

3. The Disadvantage of Grasping on to Non-Dharma

"Why is that? Once holding on to a notion of the characteristic of non-dharma, we grasp a self, a person, a sentient being, and a living being."

The characteristic of non-dharma
Generally speaking, "dharma" and "non-dharma" can be understood in two ways: (1) capitalized "Dharma" refers to the Buddhadharma, or Buddhist scriptures, and "non-Dharma" means the wrong views of heretics; (2) lowercased "dharma" means the phenomena that appear within the conventional view, and "non-dharma" indicates phenomena whose existence has been negated, or mere emptiness. Here, "non-dharma" refers to mere emptiness.

When holding on to mere emptiness, we will again fall into the four characteristics. This is because the notion of "mere emptiness" will render a belief in the existence of emptiness itself, which is the grasping on to "mine" (the characteristic of a person), which results in the grasping on to a self (the characteristic of a self), which will give rise to the continuous rebirth of a sentient being (the characteristic of a sentient being), as well as the notion of a living being who lives from birth until death (the characteristic of a living being). Therefore, a great number of Buddhist scriptures have refuted the grasping on to mere emptiness. *The Four Hundred Stanzas on the Middle Way* says, "It would be better to let the fool grasp at a self than to explain to them the theory of selflessness." This is because if people grasp the existence of a self, they can still use the view of emptiness to counteract that attachment, but if they cling to nonexistence or mere emptiness, that mistaken view is incurable. Therefore the Buddha exhorted, "You'd be better off having an attachment as gigantic as Mount Meru to 'existence' than attachment as tiny as a mustard seed to 'nonexistence.'"

A Raft Is Indispensable for Crossing a River but Must Be Left Behind Once You Reach the Other Shore

"Therefore do not hold on to dharma, do not hold on to non-dharma."

"For this reason, the Tathagata always said: 'Monks, you should understand the Dharma that I have taught is like a raft. If the Dharma has to be left behind, then what need is there to mention non-dharma?'"

We know that we have to rely on boats or rafts to cross a river, but when we reach the other shore, boats and rafts are useless. Similarly, the 84,000 Dharma teachings of the Buddha can help us to accumulate merit, purify obscurations, and reach the fruition of liberation, but at the same time, we have to avoid grasping on to the Dharma. In that case, what need is there to mention not grasping on to the non-dharma of heretics? In *Clear Words*, Bodhisattva Chandrakirti gives this good analogy: in order to scoop water, we must have a utensil, but once we have already gotten the water, the utensil is useless.

Alternatively, we can explain the latter sutra passage in this way: if we have to leave behind the Dharma within the conventional view, such as the karmic law of cause and effect that teaches us how to adopt what we should do and abandon what we should not do, there is no need to mention leaving behind the non-dharma of clinging to the nonexistence of phenomena, or mere emptiness.

Of course, before reaching liberation we should never relinquish the Dharma of conventional truth; if we do, we will lose the chance to realize the ultimate truth. Bodhisattva Nagarjuna said, "Without relying on conventional truth, it is impossible to attain the ultimate meaning." This is true to the dictum to never abandon the ship before we reach the other shore; otherwise, we would fall into the ocean and face horrendous consequences. Therefore, in the nature of ultimate reality, both Dharma and non-dharma should be relinquished; we must reside in the state of not grasping any object.

7. Unfindable and Indescribable

DO THE BUDDHA AND THE BUDDHADHARMA
EXIST INHERENTLY?

IN THE PREVIOUS chapter, it was explained that the Buddhadharma does not exist inherently but is merely the skillful means to guide sentient beings. Following that teaching, the Buddha raised another question:

"Subhuti, what do you think? Has the Tathagata attained anuttararh sammdsambodhirh? Has the Tathagata ever taught the Buddhadharma?"

This paragraph was translated by Yi Jing in this way: "Has the Tathagata realized the unsurpassable enlightenment? And has any Buddhadharma ever been taught?" Meaning: Do the merit and wisdom realized by the Tathagata exist? Does the Buddhadharma taught by the Tathagata exist? The two translators' word choices are not exactly the same, but the meaning does not differ much.

Anuttararh sammdsambodhirh
Anuttararh sammdsambodhirh is a Sanskrit term. "Anuttararh" means unsurpassable, "sammd" means perfect, and "sambodhirh" means enlightenment—that is, the perfect, unsurpassable enlightenment. In the *Oral Teaching on the Diamond Cutter Sutra*, the Sixth Patriarch explained it in this way: "A" means nonconceptual, "nuttararh" means no arrogance, "sam" means the mind always abides in meditative concentration, "md" means the mind always resides in wisdom, and "sambodhirh" means to relinquish the thoughts of ordinary beings and realize buddha nature.

It was by relying on the *Diamond Cutter Sutra* that the Sixth Patriarch reached enlightenment. There can be no doubt about this. However, his interpretation of the line is quite different from the dominant scriptures.

Khenchen Jigme Phuntsok Rinpoche said, "At times the words of some great accomplishers appeared not in accord with scriptures. Nevertheless, we should respect the vajra words of great accomplishers and take them into practice!"

BUDDHA'S WORDS ARE INDESCRIBABLE

If the Buddha had asked these questions of us, even after wasting time hemming and hawing we might not be able to utter anything. However, Subhuti was brilliant, so without hesitation he answered immediately.

Subhuti said, "From my understanding on what the Buddha has taught, there is no such dharma called anuttararh sammdsambodhirh, nor is there the Dharma taught by the Tathagata."

The *Diamond Cutter Sutra* itself says, "Anyone who wishes to meet me by form, or seek me by sound, has already entered the wrong path and would not be able to meet the Tathagata." Why does the enlightened Tathagata not exist? The Tathagata is the nature of all phenomena, rather than some particular appearance. Although the historical Buddha appeared in this world and manifested before entering parinirvana, these appearances were imputed before sentient beings in confusion and delusion; in fact, they had no inherent existence.

Why does the Buddhadharma not exist? Within the conventional view, after reaching enlightenment, Buddha Shakyamuni gave 84,000 Dharma teachings according to the capacity of individuals, but again, these teachings only appeared before sentient beings. In the ultimate view, it never occurred to the Buddha to teach the Dharma; the teachings were utterly the spontaneous display of the Buddha's wisdom power that he had appeared to turn the wheel of Dharma before sentient beings. As said in the sutra, "No single Dharma has been taught, but it appeared before sentient beings."

The above was a brief introduction; the following explains in detail the reason of "the nonexistence of the Dharma" and then the reason of "the nonexistence of the Tathagata."

PHENOMENA ARE NEITHER EXISTENT
NOR NONEXISTENT

"Why is that? What the Tathagata has taught is unfindable, indescribable, neither dharma nor non-dharma."

Unfindable, indescribable

The nature of all phenomena is the very nature of nirvana. The person who teaches the Dharma, the Dharma that has been taught, and the recipient who receives the Dharma—they are all unfindable, lacking a dualistic subject and object; everything is equal in one taste, in peace by its nature. As *The Fundamental Wisdom of the Middle Way* (chapter 21) says, "Everything is unfindable, which [fact] ceases all mental fabrication; there is neither person nor place, neither [is there] what the Buddha has ever taught."

Je Tsongkhapa also said, "Since his reaching enlightenment, the Buddha has never taught a single word, whether in the god realm or human realm, because how things ultimately abide is free from all mental fabrications, [things] like the person who is able to teach and what has been taught."

Neither dharma nor non-dharma

"Neither dharma" is the negation of dharma, or unreal things; "nor non-dharma" is the negation of non-dharma, or real functioning things. If one holds the view of mere emptiness as the ultimate reality, there would be conflicts when explaining this point. For instance, some people hold the view that "neither dharma" (unreal things) is not emptiness at the relative level and "nor non-dharma" (real functioning things) is not existent at the ultimate level, so these two entities must be analyzed alternately.

However, from our view of great emptiness, this can be easily explained. The Dharma taught by the Buddha is the negation of dharma (unreal things), so it is free from the extreme of existence; it is the negation of non-dharma (real functioning things), so it is free from the extreme of nonexistence. Therefore, ultimately speaking, Bhagavan has never taught any Buddhadharma.

This is the ultimate intended meaning of Buddha Shakyamuni.

WHAT DIFFERENTIATES BUDDHAS FROM BODHISATTVAS?

"Why is that? The noble beings are distinguished by unconditioned phenomena."

In the nature of ultimate reality, existent phenomena (real functioning things) do not exist and nonexistent phenomena (unreal things) do not exist. The nature of all phenomena is free from grasping, free from any characteristics. This has been validated by the wisdom of meditative concentration of the noble beings. The *Great Illusory Matrix* says, "The oneness of purity and equality of the basic space (dharmadhatu) has been acknowledged through noble beings' attainment of the meditative concentration of fundamental wisdom." Similarly, we also conclude the nonexistence or the lack of substantial entity of all phenomena by relying on the meditative wisdom of noble beings.

There are two aspects to meditative concentration and unconditioned phenomena. First, in the meditative concentration of the fundamental wisdom, everything is unconditioned phenomenon. Besides that, there is neither the ultimate reality nor the grasping of existence or nonexistence. Second, when noble beings enter meditative concentration, everything is the emptiness of prajna, free from all the extremes of fabrications. Vasubandhu said, "When noble beings enter meditative concentration, the distractive grasping of all conditioned phenomena ceases and the primordial wisdom of unconditioned phenomena then presents."

To explain it the other way around, if the nature of all phenomena is not unconditioned, it has to be conditioned. Kamalashila said that if the nature of all phenomena was conditioned, it must have been changing moment by moment and must be unreliable; therefore, it has to be unconditioned. If it changes according to causes and conditions, it cannot be the primordial nature of the ultimate reality of all phenomena.

Obviously, in regard to the emptiness that has been realized (object), there is no difference because the nature of the ultimate reality is unconditioned. However, in terms of the wisdom that can realize emptiness (subject), there are different degrees of profundity of the wisdom according to various capacities of sentient beings. For instance, the realization of listeners (shravakas) is less profound, the realization of bodhisattvas is more profound, and the realization of buddhas is consummate.

The Sixth Patriarch said, "Since (the practitioners of) the three vehicles have different capacities and hold different views, their realizations are different in profundity; for this reason, they are said to be different." In general, "different" is said in regard to the wisdom (subject) that can realize emptiness; as for the emptiness (object) that is to be realized, there is no difference at all. If there were, unconditioned phenomena would become impermanent.

8. Born from Buddhadharma

WHAT ARE MATERIAL OFFERINGS?

Next, the sutra explains that the merit of Dharma offerings is vast and immense, far more superior to material offerings. Especially if someone practices Dharma offerings by upholding and reciting the *Diamond Cutter Sutra*, she would amass immeasurable merit. To reach this conclusion, let's first discuss material offerings.

"Subhuti, what do you think? If someone had filled the three-thousandfold universe with the seven jewels, and made offerings with them, would this person acquire great merit?"

Subhuti said, "The merit would be great, Bhagavan. Why is that? Because merit is not merit by nature. Therefore, the Tathagata said the merit would be great."

The three-thousandfold universe

According to *Abhidharmakosha*, the four continents, the sun and moon, Mount Meru, the heavens of the desire realm, and the form realm Heaven of Brahma constitute one unit. One thousand such units constitute the one-thousandfold universe, one thousand such universes form the two-thousandfold universe, and one thousand such universes are called the "three-thousandfold universe."

The three-thousandfold universe is destroyed all at once by the fire at the end of a kalpa, and it comes into being at the same time as it is destroyed. Since these events happen to these components at the same time, they are together named as one entity.

The seven jewels

The composition of the seven jewels differ slightly in the sutras. According to the *Lotus Sutra*, they are gold, silver, lapis lazuli, musaragalva, carnelian, pearls, and roses. The *Sutra of the Buddha of Infinite Life* says they are gold, silver, lapis lazuli, crystal, coral, carnelian, and musaragalva. The *Buddha Amitabha Sutra* says they are gold, silver, lapis lazuli, crystal, musaragalva, rubies, and carnelian. The *Prajna Sutra* says gold, silver, lapis lazuli, musaragalva, carnelian, amber, and coral. And in *A Commentary on the Aspiration of Sukhavati*, Lala Sönam Chödrup (Glag bla bsod nams chos 'grub) refers them as gold, silver, lapis lazuli, crystal, obsidian, red pearl, and carnelian.

Many Buddhist sutras say: "Taking the Three Jewels as the merit field, if we make offerings of even one flower or one cup of plain water with pure motivation, the merit will be immense, so what need is there to mention that if someone offered the seven jewels filling the entire three-thousandfold universe, the merit would be immeasurable."

Why immeasurable? On the one hand, it is the merit rising from pure motivation; on the other hand, if merit did truly exist at the ultimate level, its quantity should be conceivable. However, since merit is empty, when causes and conditions are present, an illusory offering could bring illusory infinite merit.

As you may have already noticed, in the *Diamond Cutter Sutra*, views from the relative truth and the ultimate truth have often appeared in one sentence together. It is important to distinguish them as we proceed.

In general, no matter if it is merit or dharmakaya (truth body), only by relinquishing the notion of "inherent existence" can we understand genuine emptiness. Here, merit is empty at the ultimate level, but it appears as a dream or an illusion. Empty yet appearing only when causes and conditions are present is the reason for the merit to be infinite. This explanation of the material offering serves as a foil to introduce the Dharma offerings.

WHAT ARE DHARMA OFFERINGS?

"If someone else upholds this sutra, or even four lines of it, and explains it to others, the merit of this person transcends that of the former."

Worldly people often believe that the merit of material offerings is immense and that Dharma offerings could never equal it. Here, Buddha Shakyamuni said himself that the merit of Dharma offerings is far superior to the merit of material offerings! As a matter of fact, never mind offering the seven jewels filling the three-thousandfold universe, even offering a bowl of seven jewels is very difficult for us to afford. However, through the blessing of the guru and the Three Jewels, we get the chance to listen to the *Diamond Cutter Sutra*. This inconceivable merit way surpasses the merit of material offerings mentioned above, so we should be joyful.

Uphold
To uphold is to be dedicated to practicing it.

A stanza of four lines
The Sanskrit edition of the *Diamond Cutter Sutra* was originally composed in stanzas, whereas the Tibetan and Chinese editions are in prose. "A stanza of four lines" refers to a verse made up of four lines, just as in this one:

> All conditioned phenomena
> are like dreams, illusions, water bubbles,
> reflections, dewdrops, and flashes of lightning.
> View them in this way.

While upholding the *Diamond Cutter Sutra*, if we can illuminate its meaning to others, or lead others to listen to, recite, or practice it, even only one verse of it, the merit would transcend that of offering the seven jewels. As said in the *Eight Thousand Verses on Prajna*, "If a son or daughter of noble qualities could recite, uphold, or illuminate the Dharma of prajna, their merit would transcend that of any material offerings."

As we can see, the merit of Dharma offerings is immense. Once Ananda asked the Buddha, "When two people get together, what can they do to generate the greatest merit?" The Buddha said, "They can generate the maximum merit if one person teaches the Dharma and the other listens to it."

The *Lion Roar Sutra* also said, "To make offerings or give away the seven jewels filling the three-thousandfold universe could not generate the same amount of merit as illuminating a four-line verse of the Buddhadharma at the time of degeneration." The *Lotus Sutra*, the *Twenty Thousand Verses on Prajna*, and the *Sutra Requested by Sagaramati* have all praised the supreme merit of teaching the Buddhadharma, and especially the Dharma of prajna.

Therefore, on the one hand, we should cultivate the faith in emptiness explained in the Great Vehicle. On the other hand, we should introduce the sutra to more people. When people get sick or encounter unfavorable conditions, you should take that opportunity to guide them to recite the *Diamond Cutter Sutra*. In this way they will be greatly benefited in present and future lives.

THE *DIAMOND CUTTER SUTRA* GIVES BIRTH TO ALL THE BUDDHAS AND THE BUDDHADHARMA

"Why is that? Subhuti, all the buddhas and the Buddhadharma of anuttararh sammdsambodhirh arise from this sutra."

Once a lay practitioner made an offering of ten thousand dollars to a monastery. After a few decades, he still had strong attachment to the offering. When he revisited the monastery, the first thing he said was, "I made an offering of ten thousand dollars to your monastery in the year such and such. Do you still remember me?"

In some extreme examples, people even constantly mention the cookies and sweaters they have donated four or five years ago. Such offerings are not free from miserliness, attachment, and arrogance, so they are not pure offerings. If you practice and recite the *Diamond Cutter Sutra* and explain it to others, this offering of Dharma generates far more merit. Why? Because the *Diamond Cutter Sutra* interprets the emptiness of prajna, and the emptiness of prajna is the root cause of all buddhas.

The *Prajna Sutra* says, "The buddhas of the three times all have reached the perfect, unsurpassable enlightenment through prajna." In many sutras, prajna is named "the Mother of Buddhas": as the mother is the origin of children, the emptiness of prajna is the source of all buddhas.

The opening verse of *The Thirty-Seven Practices of a Bodhisattva* also says:

> The perfect buddhas, sources of benefit and happiness,
> arise from accomplishing the genuine Dharma.

Buddhahood is accomplished through the Buddhadharma, the emptiness of prajna—the source of all buddhas and bodhisattvas. Since the emptiness of prajna is the root cause of the buddhas of the three times, the Buddhadharma spread by the buddhas of the three times must be the emptiness of prajna. Otherwise, if the buddhas arise from prajna, but skip prajna and rely on something else when they help others to reach buddhahood, that would be unreasonable.

Here the text directly points out that the buddhas arise from the emptiness of prajna, and it indirectly illuminates that the Buddhadharma also originates from the emptiness of prajna. Hence, why is the merit of the *Diamond Cutter Sutra* so immense? Because it gives birth to all the buddhas and the Buddhadharma. And so, to practice, recite, and teach it can create immeasurable merit.

Buddhadharma as the Object Can Only Be Perceived by Wisdom

"Subhuti, the so-called Buddhadharma is not the Buddhadharma."

Yi Jing's translation of this passage is: "The Buddhadharma is said by the Tathagata to not be the Buddhadharma, so it is Buddhadharma." The phrasing differs, but the meaning is completely the same.

"Buddhadharma" can be explained in two ways. First, it signifies the perfect qualities of buddhas that can be realized: from the appearance, through accumulating merit by generosity and so forth, the major and minor excellent marks, the ten powers, the four fearlessnesses, and the eighteen extraordinary attributes. As said in the sutra, "The form body of the Tathagata is the body resulting from accumulating merit." However, at the ultimate level, all of these do not inherently exist. They are not the genuine, definitive Buddhadharma.

Second, the Buddhadharma refers to the nectar of sublime Dharma that can pacify sufferings. From the view of the ultimate meaning, they are not genuine Buddhadharma but only illusions within the conventional, the skillful means used by the Buddha to liberate sentient beings. The genuine Buddhadharma is free from all conceptual elaboration or extremes—it is the great unconditioned phenomenon.

The Sixth Patriarch once said, "Buddhist sutras are not genuine Buddhadharma; they can be perceived by ordinary-flesh eyes, so they are not the ultimate. Genuine Buddhadharma as the object can only be perceived by wisdom."

9. One Characteristic, No Characteristic

THE PREVIOUS CHAPTER illuminated the merit of the *Diamond Cutter Sutra* by comparing the merit of material offerings and Dharma offerings. Next, the sutra says it is indispensable to realize emptiness in order to achieve the four attainments of shramana.

WHAT ARE THE FOUR ATTAINMENTS OF SHRAMANA?

The noble fruits of the Basic Vehicle are the four attainments of shramana or the eight attainments of shramana. The four attainments of shramana include the sotapanna, sakadagami, anagami, and arhat, or stream-enterer, once-returner, non-returner, and arhat. The eight attainments of shramana are the path to stream-entry and the fruition of stream-entry, the path to once-returning and the fruition of once-returning, the path to non-returning and the fruition of non-returning, and the path to arhatship and the fruition of arhatship. "Path" means the way to the goal, before attaining the actual fruition. "Fruition" indicates one has transcended ordinary beings; one becomes the noble being with certain realizations and the actual attainment.

No matter which fruition they have attained, practitioners must first realize the emptiness of no characteristics and no grasping. Without abandoning grasping to the inherent existence of phenomena, one is no different from ordinary beings. The *Prajnaparamita Sutra* says, "Anyone who holds inherent existence would never reach the liberation of the three levels of enlightenment." Mipham Rinpoche also said, "Shravakas (listeners) or pratyeka buddhas (self-realized buddhas) must realize the emptiness of phenomena emphasized in the Great Vehicle. Without realizing the emptiness of phenomena, one cannot reach the attainment of stream-entry, let alone transcend the three realms." The following text will expound on these points.

GENUINE ATTAINMENT OF STREAM-ENTRY CAN ONLY BE REACHED WHEN THERE IS NO ATTACHMENT TOWARD FORM, SOUND, TASTE, SMELL, TOUCH, OR DHARMAS

"Subhuti, what do you think? Does 'I have attained sotapanna' ever occur to a sotapanna?

Subhuti said, "No, Bhagavan. Why? Sotapanna is named a stream-enterer, but there is no being who has entered. Not entering form, sound, smell, taste, touch, and dharma is the reason for naming sotapanna."

Sotapanna

Sotapanna is also called the "attainment of stream-entry." It is categorized as the "path of seeing" in the Basic Vehicle rather than in the Great Vehicle. Once this attainment is reached, one has become a noble being, so it is called "the beginning of the noble being." Since it is the first noble fruition of the Shravaka Vehicle, it is also named the "first fruition."

In the text, the Buddha said "sotapanna is entry" at one time and "sotapanna is not entry" at another time. A number of scholars are at a loss to reconcile the apparent contradiction. In fact, if you remember to explain the statement with the two truths, the problem can be easily solved. Conventionally, it is acceptable to establish the name and characteristic and admit that sotapanna transcends the state of ordinary beings and indicates entry into the stream of the noble beings; but ultimately, nothing of the fruition attainer, the fruition being attained, and the fact of attaining fruition truly exists. Since there are no such things that can be relied on or that are able to respond, there would be no grasping to the inherent existence of the six sensory objects (form, sound, smell, taste, touch, and dharma). This, then, is the genuine state of sotapanna, or the attainment of stream-entry. Therefore, the first stage of the Basic Vehicle, sotapanna, also requires relinquishing attachment; otherwise, one has no chance to realize the truth or reach the path of seeing. In his *Commentary on the Sixty Stanzas of Reasoning*, Je Tsongkhapa also cited this line from the *Diamond Cutter Sutra* and explained it in this way.

The Attainment of Once-Returning Requires Not to Grasp Coming or Going

"Subhuti, what do you think? Does it occur to a sakadagami, 'I have attained sakadagami'?"

Subhuti said, "No, Bhagavan. Why? Sakadagami is named 'once-returning,' but there is actually no coming or going, so it is called 'sakadagami.'"

Sakadagami

Sakadagami is also called the "attainment of once-returning," which is the second stage of the Basic Vehicle. This fruition is free from the first six of the nine stages of afflictive emotions on the path of practice in the desire realm, but has not yet relinquished the afflictive emotions of the upper three stages. As a result, they will come back to the human realm or the sixth heaven of the desire realm one more time. Therefore they are named "once-returners."

Although within the conventional once-returners have to come back to take rebirth in the desire realm one more time, in ultimate reality they have realized the prajnaparamita, or wisdom of selflessness, and are free from the concept of "I am coming" or "I am going." As said in *The Fundamental Wisdom of the Middle Way*, "If there is no I, how can there be mine? When I and mine are destroyed, the grasping to I and mine vanishes." Therefore, once realizing the emptiness of selflessness, one would surely relinquish the grasping to coming or going.

What Is the Attainment of Non-returning?

"Subhuti, what do you think? Does it ever occur to an anagami, 'I have attained anagami'?"

Subhuti said, "No, Bhagavan. Why? Anagami is named 'non-returning,' but there is actually no returning, so it is called 'anagami.'"

Anagami

Anagami is also named the "attainment of non-returning, non-coming." It is the third fruition of the Basic Vehicle. Since noble beings at this stage can abide in form or formless realms without returning to the desire realm to take rebirth, they are named "non-returners." As described for the first two stages, non-returning within the conventional means not coming back to take rebirth in the desire realm, but when examined by ultimate analysis, neither returning nor non-returning are findable.

Theoretically, in Buddhist sutras we should expect disciples to raise questions and Buddha Shakyamuni to give answers. However, sometimes their roles are switched. In this sutra, most often it was Buddha Shakyamuni who asked questions and Subhuti who answered, and then the Buddha only confirmed or validated the response. The *Heart Sutra* is another example. We see that Buddhist sutras can be directly said by the Buddha himself, or they could be said by other figures first and then only verified by the Buddha.

Why Is an Arhat Called a "Foe Destroyer"?

"Subhuti, what do you think? Does it ever occur to an arhat, 'I have attained arhathood'?"

Subhuti said, "No, Bhagavan. Why? There is no such dharma called 'arhat' truly existing."

Arhat

Arhat is the highest attainment in the Basic Vehicle; this attainment has transcended cyclic existence. In the context of the Great Vehicle, this highest attainment of the Basic Vehicle is not consummate because subtle cognitive obscurations still remain at this stage.

The Sanskrit "arhat" is translated as *dgra bcom pa* in Tibetan. The literal meaning is "foe destroyer," indicating that at this stage all the enemies of afflictive emotions have been conquered, though the enemies of cognitive obscurations (the grasping to the three spheres) have not yet been defeated. However, since arhats have already relinquished the eighty-one types of afflictive emotions on the path of practice, they have been liberated from samsara. So in this sense they are foe destroyers.

In the Basic Vehicle, arhathood is the highest attainment, but according to the *Lotus Sutra* and Mipham Rinpoche's *Beacon of Certainty*, in the end an arhat has to leave the Basic Vehicle for the Great Vehicle in order to achieve higher realization. However, some people confuse the Great Vehicle with the Basic Vehicle and believe an arhat has already attained the tolerance of non-arising phenomena, a fruition achieved at the eighth ground of bodhisattvas. People who hold this view might have read neither the *Abhidharmakosha* nor learned the *Ornament of Clear Realization*, so their understanding contradicts Buddhist doctrines.

Here Subhuti was very confident that an arhat would never grasp, "I am an arhat." Why? Because in ultimate reality an arhat has completely destroyed the five aggregates and relinquished the conceptualization of mind consciousness. This has been described by the Basic Vehicle. Similarly, the Great Vehicle stated in *The Introduction to the Middle Way*:

> The nature of phenomena, enshrouded by our ignorance, is
>   "all-concealed,"
> but what this ignorance contrives appears as true.
> And so the Buddha spoke of "all-concealing truth,"
> and thus contrived, phenomena are "all-concealing."
> (chapter 6, verse 28)

Due to the obscuration of ignorance, ordinary beings hold conventional appearance to exist inherently, so it is called "the conventional truth" or "the relative truth." However, for arhats, buddhas, and bodhisattvas, since the grasping to inherent existence has been completely destroyed, all the dependently imputed phenomena are called "convention," but not "truth." Therefore, during post-meditative concentration, arhats are aware they are arhats but they do not grasp it as existing inherently.

WHAT WOULD GO WRONG IF AN ARHAT THINKS, "I'VE ATTAINED ARHATSHIP"

"Bhagavan, if an arhat thought, 'I have attained arhatship,' he must have had the conception of a self, a person, a sentient being, and a living being."

When an arhat has the notion of "I am an arhat," that is the conception of a self. Knowing "I am an arhat" and others are ordinary beings is the conception of a person. Thinking that so many sentient beings in cyclic existence of the three realms have not yet attained arhatship is the conception of a sentient being. Pondering over the future when I, this arhat, enter the meditative concentration of cessation and dissolve into the basic space (dharmadhatu) is the conception of a living being.

Therefore, once the notion of "I have attained arhatship" arises, the four graspings follow immediately. As said in *The Introduction to the Middle Way*, the root cause of cyclic existence for every sentient being is the grasping to a self and the grasping to mine. If arhats have not yet relinquished these graspings, they are no different from ordinary beings. How, then, could they be arhats?

A GENUINE ARHAT WOULD NEVER THINK, "I AM THE MOST SUPREME AMONG PEOPLE, I AM MARVELOUS"

"Bhagavan, the Buddha said I have attained the samadhi of non-contention, I am the most supreme among humans, number one among arhats who are free from desire."

The samadhi of non-contention

The samadhi of non-contention is called "the meditative absorption of non-affliction" in the Tibetan version and "abiding in non-contention" in both Xuan Zang and Yi Jing's translations.

As said in the *Avatamsaka Sutra*, "Contention is cyclic existence, whereas non-contention is nirvana." The *Abhidharmakosha* points out that, due to their desire for enjoyment, householders constantly dispute with others in regard to property, land, livestock, and spouses. Due to their partiality toward their own lineage or tradition, monastics fiercely debate. No matter if they are religious believers or secular people, as long as they are entangled in disputes, it is difficult for them to maintain healthy interpersonal relationships, let alone attain unsurpassable nirvana. It is not uncommon to see two people in great harmony today turn into irreconcilable enemies tomorrow.

The *Nirvana Sutra* sums it up well: "When there is freedom from conceptual thoughts, there is no contention regarding any phenomena." Only when the grasping of conceptual thoughts is entirely pacified can all dispute and contention be dispelled and the state of Subhuti attained.

The most supreme among humans

The ten great disciples of the Buddha are all arhats, but each of them has a specific strength in their state of realization. For instance, Kashyapa is number one in dhuta, or austerity, Shariputra is number one in wisdom,

Maudgalyayana is number one in miraculous power, Purna is number one in teaching the Dharma, Ananda is number one in extensive listening to the Dharma, Subhuti is number one in explaining the view of emptiness (or number one in being free from desire). All these qualities can be called "the most supreme among humans."

Number one among arhats who are free from desire

Here "free from desire" refers to being free from all sorts of afflictive emotions. Arhats have all been freed from any mental afflictions, but according to scriptures of the Basic Vehicle, their realizations vary in terms of profundity, so Subhuti has been ranked the most supreme among all the arhats.

In the conventional sense, Subhuti has the most profound understanding of the emptiness of prajnaparamita, so every time he expresses his experience, the Buddha commends him, "Thus it is, thus it is," fully agreeing with his views. The Buddha also declared in public, in accordance with the capacities of various disciples: "Among the ten great disciples of mine, Subhuti is number one being free from desire and explaining emptiness." However, this is said only in the conventional sense, as a genuine arhat would never have the abhimana, or prideful attachment, of "I," thinking, "I am number one among humans and I am marvelous."

The following is an analysis of the realization of arhats at the ultimate level.

"FORM IS EMPTINESS, EMPTINESS IS FORM"

"It never occurs to me that I am an arhat free from desire. Bhagavan, if I have the thought, 'I have attained arhatship,' the Bhagavan would never say, 'Subhuti is the one who enjoys aranya,' or, 'It is because Subhuti does not engage in any act that Subhuti is named "the one who enjoys aranya".'"

Though the appearance of arhats varies dramatically, all of them have relinquished the grasping to I or mine. As said in the *Uttara Tantra Shastra*, a Mahayana bodhisattva can manifest and experience all sorts of suffering, such as birth, aging, sickness, and death. However, in their true state of realization, they do not have even the slightest attachment that ordinary beings have.

If you have understood that emptiness is dependent origination, you will find that there is no conflict among all phenomena, but only profound meaning.

The one who enjoys aranya

"Enjoy" is to like; *aranya* (wilderness) is a peaceful place, in contrast to urban areas (*grama*). "The one who enjoys *aranya*" means someone who likes to stay in peaceful places. Here "peaceful" signifies peaceful body, speech, and mind—the state in which afflictive emotions have been pacified. In the Basic Vehicle, this can be achieved only by arhats. So the most supreme arhat is the most peaceful being.

Ordinary people are not peaceful but are continually muddle-headed and distracted. We bustle about all day in body, speech, and mind, longing for fame and gain. Only by relinquishing the grasping to self can enlightenment be reached. Only by understanding the selflessness of phenomena can the noble path be realized, whereby one attains arhatship and becomes the most peaceful one.

In the *Beacon of Certainty*, seven scriptural authorities and three methods of reasoning have been applied to show that in order to reach arhatship, one must realize the selflessness of phenomena. In fact, the *Diamond Cutter Sutra* can also prove this statement: If arhats have not yet realized the selflessness of phenomena but only the selflessness of a person, they would fall into the extreme of existence; therefore, they must have at least a partial realization that dependent origination is emptiness.

In the ultimate reality Subhuti has never grasped the notion that he is number one among all arhats for relinquishing desire, but within the conventional, the Buddha did commend him this way. The Buddha's commendation demonstrates the theory of "form is emptiness, emptiness is form." The principle of dependent origination can only be thoroughly comprehended by the Buddha; it is extremely difficult for ordinary people to understand. Yet without understanding it, even world-famous masters cannot realize the noble path.

As Bodhisattva Nagarjuna said in his *Treatise on Transcending the Mundane World*, not having realized the ultimate reality, ordinary people mentally fabricate an arising from self, arising from other, arising from both self and other, and arising without a cause. As a result, they inevitably experience various kinds of suffering. On the contrary, as the Buddha taught, arising upon causes and conditions is actually the only truth of the entire universe, the natural law of all phenomena. Realizing this, one can transcend all sufferings.

Therefore, understanding the principle that dependent origination is emptiness is of the utmost importance. Once we understand it, we would know that Subhuti has no grasping in ultimate reality, but in the dreamlike and illusory state of appearances, it is acceptable to call him "number one in relinquishing desire."

10. Adorn Pure Land

IN THE PREVIOUS chapter, it was said that noble beings at the four stages in the Basic Vehicle have all relinquished attachment to their attainment. Next, the sutra says that the prophecy received by the Buddha, the material world transformed by him, and the sentient world liberated by him all lack inherent existence.

There is a correlation between these three: within the conventional, the Buddha first received a prophecy, then he transformed and resided in the pure land, and finally he liberated countless sentient beings (the sentient world).

TO OBTAIN THE DHARMA IS A CONCEPTUAL THOUGHT THAT SHOULD BE FORSAKEN

The Buddha asked Subhuti, "What do you think? In the past, has the Tathagata received any Dharma before Buddha Dipankara?"

"No, Bhagavan. The Tathagata has not obtained any Dharma before Buddha Dipankara."

Subhuti's negative answers seem to perfectly suit every question raised by the Buddha. Of course at the ultimate level what Subhuti said is true, but within the conventional, Buddha Shakyamuni had indeed received the Dharma.

As recorded in the *Sutra of the Virtuous Kalpa*, ninety-one kalpas ago, a previous reincarnation of Buddha Shakyamuni was called the "Youth Dharma Cloud"; he had obtained the forbearance of non-arising phenomena, an attainment of the eighth stage of bodhisattvas. Then Buddha Dipankara prophesized, "In the virtuous kalpa after ninety-one kalpas, you will become a Buddha (the fourth Buddha) in Saha world (Sahalokadhatu), named Shakyamuni."

Therefore, within the conventional, Buddha Shakyamuni had indeed received prophecy and the Dharma in the presence of Buddha Dipankara, and had attained the forbearance of non-arising phenomena. However, in ultimate reality, this entire event does not exist inherently. There is no Dharma to be received, no person who can receive it, and no sign indicating it has been received. Both the object and the subject are originally empty in nature.

Vasubandhu said, "To obtain the Dharma is a conceptual thought that should be forsaken." Other scriptures also say, "If a bodhisattva has the notion 'I have received prophecy,' that prophecy is not a genuine prophecy but a prophecy given by demons." Our guru Jigme Phuntsok Rinpoche has also admonished us in this way: "If you believe you have received a prophecy that guarantees your accomplishment with no further diligence, such arrogance and grasping have already shown this prophecy is not authentic." The Sixth Patriarch also says, "The Buddhadharma is as vast as the sunlight that pervades everywhere. It does not have the subject of obtaining nor the object of being obtained, so it is unattainable." Although he expresses the idea slightly differently from other teachers, the ultimate meaning is the same.

In general, ultimately, Buddha Shakyamuni has never received prophecy or Dharma in the presence of Buddha Dipankara, but conventionally, we have to admit he did. If we don't distinguish the meaning based on the two truths, you will think the Buddha's stories in the sutras are inconsistent. So it is indispensable to distinguish the ultimate and conventional truths in the *Diamond Cutter Sutra*!

Besides Pure Mind, There Is No Pure Land in This World

"Subhuti, what do you think? Do bodhisattvas adorn the buddhafield?"

"No, Bhagavan. Why? Adorning the buddhafield is not adorning, so it is called 'adorning.'"

All the bodhisattvas, from the first to the tenth stages, need to create and adorn their fields. For instance, at his causal stage, Buddha Shakyamuni made five hundred great aspirations in order to reside and uphold the Saha world (Sahalokadhatu) in the future. When he was Bhikshu Dharmakara, Buddha Amitabha made forty-eight great aspirations in order to reside and uphold the Pure Land of Great Bliss in the future. Medicine Buddha also made twelve great aspirations to reside and uphold the Vaidurya world in the future.

Based on the views in *The Ornament of Clear Realization*, at the three pure stages, from the eighth to the tenth stages, bodhisattvas need to create pure lands. Therefore, conventionally speaking, bodhisattvas have to adorn their fields.

This is also true for many practitioners today. While they are studying in a Buddhist institute, they keep in touch with lay practitioners and monks in cities because they are preparing to establish Dharma centers so that when they finish studying, they will have a place to spread the Dharma and benefit sentient beings. Likewise, when bodhisattvas reach buddhahood, they also need buddhafields; otherwise, their great vows and aspirations to liberate sentient beings might be difficult. Therefore, within the conventional, all these do exist.

However, Subhuti's negative answer is based on the ultimate truth. When we say bodhisattvas adorn buddhafields, in ultimate reality, the subject of adorning the field does not exist, the object of being adorned does not exist, and the appearance of adorning does not exist. If they exist inherently, they must exist in the form of particles in the material world. However, if examined with the wisdom of the ultimate truth, neither particles nor material world can be found.

Therefore, as sutras that have a definitive meaning in Sutrayana, such as the *Vimalakirti Sutra*, say, "As the mind is pure, the field is pure." Within the conventional, as long as a mind is pure, all the appearances perceived by it must also be pure. In the eyes of the Brahma King who has a conch-shaped tuft of hair, the Saha world is also a pure land. However, examining this further, at the ultimate level, there is no single inherent particle in any field. All appearances are the projection of primordial purity.

Not adorning

It is also frequently quoted in Chan Buddhism, "The nature of mind is a pure seat of enlightenment; besides pure mind, there is no pure land out there."

In general, scriptures that possess definitive meaning have revealed that ultimately, when the mind is pure, the land is pure. Besides that, there is no truly existing Vaidurya world, Saha world, or Pure Land of Great Bliss, and so forth. Within the conventional, these worlds are acceptable, but in ultimate reality, adorning fields does not exist. This is the connotation of "not adorning."

It is called "adorning"

What does "it is called 'adorning'" mean? At the conventional level, all these fields exist; just like in a dream, we can say, "I have spent a happy morning in the garden." Conventionally, adorning fields exist like dreams or illusions. With illusion-like aspiration, bodhisattvas adorn illusion-like fields, finally attain illusion-like fruition, and liberate illusion-like sentient beings. All these are reasonable.

GIVE RISE TO PURE MIND WITHOUT FIXATING ON ANYTHING

"Therefore, Subhuti, bodhisattva mahasattvas should give rise to pure mind without fixating on form, sound, smell, taste, touch, and dharma; they should give rise to pure mind without fixating on anything."

They should give rise to pure mind without fixating on anything

The Sixth Patriarch realized enlightenment based on the last few words of this paragraph, *"they should give rise to pure mind without fixating on anything."* In the past, the Fifth Patriarch encouraged followers to recite and practice nothing more than the *Diamond Cutter Sutra.* He taught the illiterate to recite "Maha Prajna Paramita," which represents the *Diamond Cutter Sutra.* This prayer means transcendental wisdom that reaches the other shore, or the perfection of wisdom. The perfection of wisdom includes all the Prajnaparamita sutras, which in turn can be summarized in the one-line prayer "Maha Prajna Paramita." In Chinese Buddhism today, people still follow this tradition: the illiterate elders recite "Amitabha" in the Pure Land tradition or "Maha Prajna Paramita" in the Chan tradition.

Bodhisattva mahasattvas should give rise to pure mind without attaching to external objects, discriminating "this is white, that is red" or "this is rectangular, that is triangular." All these thoughts are attachment. Likewise, giving rise to thoughts based on sound, smell, taste, touch, or dharma is also attachment that should be abandoned. We should give rise to pure mind without fixating on anything, just as the *Ornament of Clear Realization* says, being free from the grasper and the grasped.

The Sixth Patriarch attained enlightenment based on the line quoted at the start of this section because it summarizes the most supreme meaning of the Middle Way. From my understanding, "without fixating on anything" is said from the aspect of emptiness: all phenomena are free of object and subject and not different from empty space, so we should give up thinking they exist inherently. "Give rise to pure mind" is to emphasize that while all phenomena are empty, their appearance is unceasing and wisdom is able to arise from emptiness.

The Introduction to the Middle Way says that all phenomena are empty by nature but can appear vividly in emptiness. Therefore, the line we are analyzing has examined the utmost secret meaning of the Middle Way— the nondual nature of emptiness and appearance. Regarding emptiness, it agrees with the view in *The Six Treatises of the Middle Way* by Bodhisattva Nagarjuna; regarding appearances, it is not different from the principles of the Mahayana *Uttara Tantra Shastra* by Bodhisattva Maitreya. The nature of mind is emptiness, but the display of wisdom has never ceased—this is the ultimate reality.

Therefore, based on my understanding, "without fixating on anything" is the great emptiness and "give rise to the mind" is the great luminosity. According to the Great Perfection, "without fixating on anything" is primordial purity and "give rise to the mind" is spontaneous presence. From the Sutrayana point of view, "without fixating on anything" is the intended meaning of the second turning of the wheel of Dharma and "give rise to the mind" is the secret meaning of the third turning of the wheel of Dharma. Based on this single line, one can completely realize the nature of mind.

After the Sixth Patriarch attained enlightenment, while confirming his realization, the Fifth Patriarch once said, "Without realizing the nature of mind, there is no benefit to study the Dharma. Once you realize the nature of mind, and see the nature of yourself, you can be called the 'Great Man,' the 'Guide of Human and Gods,' the 'Buddha.'"

We should savor carefully these supreme vajra words. Especially for those who have great faith in the *Diamond Cutter Sutra*, if you master the profound connotations of the text, you would have a chance to attain enlightenment.

THE WISE NEVER ATTACH TO THE BODIES
IN A DREAM

"Subhuti, if someone has a body as giant as Mount Meru, do you think this body is giant?"

Subhuti, "Giant, indeed, Bhagavan. Why? The Buddha said it is not a body, so it is named a 'giant body.'"

Subhuti's answer is excellent! The bodies of sentient beings are made up of aggregates. Sentient beings all have different bodies, even those as small as crickets and ants are different. If a sentient being has a body as huge as Mount Meru, such a body could be said to be gigantic at the conventional level,[5] but in the ultimate meaning, all phenomena are empty in nature, so there is no difference in terms of the size of any body.

The Buddha's question aimed to dispel the heretics' wrong views of the intrinsic existence of phenomena. Some heretics believe that the creator of material and sentient worlds is a great lord. His body is gigantic, solid, unchanging, and everlasting. Within the conventional, if someone's body is as huge as described earlier, we have to admit it is giant. But at the ultimate level, body is just one of the aggregates—the aggregate of form. When examined closely, the so-called giant does not exist inherently.

Subhuti said, *"The Buddha said it is not a body, so it is named a giant body."* Only when there is no fixed form and body is it actually a giant body. *Guide to the Bodhisattva's Way of Life* also examined the ultimate reality that bodies are empty in nature and that there is not even one single particle at the ultimate level. "Therefore, among wise people, who would attach to a dreamlike body?" was the conclusion. A genuine wise person would never attach to a dreamlike body. After all, no matter how tall or big a body is in a dream, it is just an illusory appearance.

Terton Lerab Lingpa once saw a noble being who was as tall as a three- or four-storied building around Serthar Stupa, but in ultimate reality, such a body is only as real as a dream. Since anything arising through causes and conditions is not real, and bodies also arise from causes and conditions, they must be empty in nature.

The supreme view of the Buddha is that bodies transcend any conceptual category of "size"; in the ultimate meaning, they are empty by nature. Vasubandhu also said, "Relying on the conventional truth, the dreamlike body can be admitted; but relying on the ultimate truth, not even a particle of the body exists."

Again, when studying the *Diamond Cutter Sutra*, we must be sure to distinguish the two truths. Without examination, bodies, buddhafields, and all phenomena seemingly exist. However, through close examination we see that all phenomena lack inherent existence and are empty by nature. After concluding that one body does not exist inherently, we can infer that the bodies of all sentient beings in cyclic existence do not exist inherently. If bodies do not exist, how can various behaviors that rely on bodies exist?

11. Unconditioned Merit Is More Supreme

"Subhuti, if there are as many Ganges rivers as the number of sand grains in the Ganges River, what do you think? Would the sand grains in all these Ganges rivers be many?"

Subhuti answered, "A great many, Bhagavan. The number of Ganges rivers in total is already numerous, let alone the sand in them."

"Subhuti, let me tell you with true speech: If a son or daughter of noble qualities makes offerings with the seven jewels that fill up the three-thousandfold universe that are as numerous as the number of sand grains in all these Ganges rivers, would the merit be great?"

Subhuti answered, "Great, Bhagavan."

The Buddha told Subhuti, "If a son or daughter of noble qualities upheld and explained this sutra, or even one verse of four lines from it, to others, the merit would surpass the merit of the former jewel offerings."

The Ganges

THE GANGES arises from the western Himalayas and is one of the largest rivers in Asia. It has been said that its origin is an elephant-like mountain, and that streams of clear water gush out from the mouth of the elephant. Merging with numerous rivers, it flows through India and Bangladesh and finally enters the Indian Ocean.

Indian linguists (Tib. *rigne sgra*) believe that drinking the water in the Ganges can unlock one's inner wisdom. Nirgrantha followers believe that bathing in the Ganges can purify one's obscurations. There is a moving story about the Ganges in the minor science of synonyms (Tib. *rigne mngon brjod*). Once, Brahma sent a goddess to the human realm. This goddess was too shy to appear as a beautiful lady herself, so she decided to appear in the form of a river that flows from the hair of a risis (human holy beings partly in heaven) named Drapel. So the Ganges is often called "Brahma Beauty" or "Celestial River." The Ganges frequently appears in Buddhist sutras as a trope to posit a number that is too big to be counted.

A famous writer in the thirteenth century in Tibet once claimed that in Buddhist sutras the sand grains in the Ganges can be explained in two ways. One is the sand grains on the riverbank of the Ganges specifically; the other is the sand grains on ocean beaches in general. In the past, when I accompanied His Holiness Jigme Phuntsok Rinpoche to India, we also visited the Ganges, and found the sand grains in this river are not different from sand in an ocean beach. Some spots have lots of sand and at some sites we can barely see any. There were many Nirgrantha followers bathing in the river every single day.

Nevertheless, the merit to make offerings of the seven jewels, filling as many three-thousandfold universes as there are grains of sand in the Ganges, is far beyond our imagination. Put aside the seven jewels filling even one three-thousandfold universe, practicing generosity by giving away inferior materials or a small amount of wealth can also create great merit.

The Precious Garland of the Middle Way says, "To give away some inferior materials to a beggar now will result in receiving one hundredfold of what you have given away in a future lifetime." Even giving away insignificant stuff to a beggar, you are going to attain one hundredfold of merit in a future lifetime. Therefore, anyone having faith in the words of the Buddha can understand that the merit of material offerings is inconceivable.

However, when compared with the Dharma offering of reciting and practicing the *Diamond Cutter Sutra*, the merit of material offerings is not worth mentioning. This principle has often been addressed in sutras. This is because Dharma offerings relate to the perfection of wisdom, which is the root cause that dispels the darkness of ignorance of sentient beings, whereas material offerings can only meet the need of sentient beings temporarily, providing enough food and clothes for this life but unable to uproot the ignorance that obscures the minds of sentient beings from life to life. However, some people hold the opposite view. They place great importance on material offerings and completely neglect Dharma offerings.

Vasubandhu has summarized the merit of reciting and upholding the *Diamond Cutter Sutra* in these four points: (1) to obtain vast merit; (2) to be able to accomplish difficult tasks (it is impossible for an ordinary being to make offerings of the seven jewels filling the three-thousandfold universe; however, an ordinary being can recite the *Diamond Cutter Sutra* one time, and this creates far more merit); (3) to be respected by celestial beings; and (4) to attain the same body as the Buddha's. The latter two points will be explained later; here let's explain the first two.

To recite and uphold the *Diamond Cutter Sutra* can create vast merit that results from the inconceivable power of dependent origination. How does the power of dependent origination work? The Buddha's instructions have great power; if one can put them into practice, even one insignificant virtuous deed, the benefit will be immense.

As said in the *Kshitigarbha Sutra*, "In the future, if a son or daughter of noble qualities can plant virtuous roots in the Buddhadharma, or practice generosity and offerings, or improve and fix stupas or temples, or bind and neaten sutras, even if it is as insignificant as a string, a particle, a sand grain, or a drop, as long as these virtuous deeds are dedicated to dharma-dhatu, the merit of this person will let him or her enjoy supreme happiness in hundreds and thousands of lifetimes."

The *Buddha Family Sutra* also says, "For the Guide Buddha, even by doing some insignificant good deed, one will be born in the higher realms for a long time and attain enlightenment later." To recite the *Diamond Cutter Sutra* is an easy task, but the merit accumulated by doing so is inconceivable. We should not have the slightest doubt about it. The sutra is the vajra words of the Buddha.

In the Tang dynasty there was a man who had recited the *Diamond Cutter Sutra* his entire life. In his later years, he suffered from leprosy and nobody dared to take care of him. His family sent him to a quiet, remote mountain, leaving him and leaving his disease to run its course. He sat alone, awaiting the arrival of death. Seeing his own body rot off piece by piece made him extremely sad. One day a tiger came close. At first the man was terrified, but suddenly he recalled a four-line verse in the *Diamond Cutter Sutra*, so he kept reciting this verse with his eyes tightly closed. As the tiger approached him and licked the wounds on his body, he trembled with great fear. After a while, the tiger left quietly, and when the man opened his eyes, to his great surprise, all the wounds had completely healed.

Therefore we should never underestimate the merit of the *Diamond*

Cutter Sutra. Even reciting four lines of it can dispel immeasurable suffering and bring infinite merit. This is not a legend, but the undeceiving vajra words of the Buddha. If we can recite the sutra wholeheartedly, we will eventually attain enlightenment.

12. Venerating the Sublime Dharma

"Again, Subhuti, whoever explains this sutra, or even one four-line verse, at a place, this place would be venerated by gods, humans, and asuras as if it was a buddha stupa or temple. Moreover, if someone can uphold and recite it, Subhuti, this person would have accomplished the supreme, unsurpassable, rare Dharma."

THE LITERAL MEANING of this paragraph is straightforward. However, without further analyzing its content, people who don't have good training in understanding sutras and shastras often have doubts: "How come a place where the *Diamond Cutter Sutra* exists is the same as a place where buddhas reside?" "Why should we respect the *Diamond Cutter Sutra* reciters as if they were stupas or temples?" Therefore it is very necessary to study the scripture authorities in Buddhist sutras and shastras.

Here the Buddha has explained to Subhuti the supreme merit of this sutra. What kind of merit? According to the view of Kumarajiva and the understanding of many great masters in Han Chinese areas, wherever and whenever, whether by lay practitioners or monastics, as long as this sutra is explained, even only a four-line verse of it, the spot becomes a merit field, like a stupa for all the nagas and rakshasas.

This passage can be explained in two ways: (1) after a person explains the *Diamond Cutter Sutra*, that place becomes the merit field, and (2) this person becomes the merit field—that is, sentient beings should respect the sutra instructor as if he were a stupa.

Here "explains" is often understood as "to teach," not as reciting. It gives the impression that reciting the *Diamond Cutter Sutra* does not create the same merit. However, according to the Tibetan edition, besides the word "explain" there is also "recite," which means that no matter if one recites by oneself or explains to other people, as little as a four-line verse, the site has already become a genuine Buddhist stupa or temple, so all the gods and humans should pay respect. From my understanding, the Tibetan edition has a wider perspective.

Why does it create such great merit?

1. The *Diamond Cutter Sutra* explains the emptiness of prajnaparamita, which is the birth place of all the buddhas and the perfect, unsurpassable enlightenment.

2. In the *Ear Adornment Sutra*, the Buddha said, "In the last five hundred years of the degeneration time, I will appear as words; you should view words as me and show respect." So in the degeneration time, the buddha appears in the world as words. If this is the case, the *Diamond Cutter Sutra* is of course Buddha Shakyamuni; if we pay respect to it, we are bound to gain blessing.

3. People who recite and uphold the *Diamond Cutter Sutra* are no different from the bodies of the Buddha.

4. People who recite and uphold the *Diamond Cutter Sutra* are messengers sent by the Buddha to uphold the enlightened activities of the Tathagata.

Therefore, a Kadampa master once said, "When there is a prajna sutra, buddha stupa, and buddha statue in one's home, this home has already become a genuine temple."

Wherever the *Diamond Cutter Sutra* resides, all the gods and Dharma protectors do their utmost to protect this place. Toward the end of the Tang dynasty, a man found a place vast and pure, so he wrote the *Diamond Cutter Sutra* joyfully on the ground. In time, the scripts gradually disappeared, but the gods still protected that place day and night. Every time it rained, snowed, or hailed, the ground was wet except for the spot where the *Diamond Cutter Sutra* was transcribed.

Local villagers often came here to seek shelter from the rain. In time, it happened that a monk with some realization examined the place when he entered meditative concentration and found someone had transcribed the *Diamond Cutter Sutra* on the ground, so gods had protected it from the rain. If people, not knowing this, trampled on it, they would create vast fault. So he persuaded local villagers to stop seeking shelter from the rain at that spot.

Not only can transcribing the *Diamond Cutter Sutra* create immense merit, but one can also gain inconceivable experience by carrying it around with faith. In the Tang dynasty there was a man who kept the *Diamond Cutter Sutra* in the pocket of his upper garment; every time demons attempted to harm him, they failed. Once his enemy tried to shoot him with an arrow—the arrow penetrated to his heart, but it could not go through his heart and left no wound.

Of course, some people may not believe in such merit through stories passed down to us. So it is necessary to use scriptural authorities to support the fact that the *Diamond Cutter Sutra* is no different from the Buddha himself. Moreover, when we recite sutras, we are bound to recall the Buddha. Once we recall the Buddha, the Buddha is bound to appear before us. As the *King of Meditative Concentration* says, "Whoever recollects the Buddha, the Buddha will always reside before him."

Uphold and recite

"Uphold and recite" is used in Kumarajiva's edition. Xuan Zang's translation is in accord with the Tibetan edition, which has "transcribe, uphold, recite, master, as well as explain, teach, and meditate according to its meaning." The latter translation is more comprehensive. If someone recites, upholds, or transcribes a four-line verse of the *Diamond Cutter Sutra*, the merit is indescribable. Obviously, if one could master the meaning of the entire sutra and meditate with correct understanding, the merit is even more immense.

This has been well explained by Master Han Shan in the *Vajra Destroying All Doubts* (Chin. *Jin Gang Jue Yi*): "Since a four-line verse is the entire dharmakaya, it is no different from the Buddha remaining in this world and teaching disciples." If practicing only one four-line verse can create such immense merit, mastering the entire *Diamond Cutter Sutra* is bound to accomplish the unsurpassable Dharma and allow the attainment of buddhahood. This feat is as rare as lotus flowers blooming in fire.

Moreover, wherever the sutras reside is the place where the Buddha is. This is because on the one hand, in the time of degeneration the Buddha appears as words and scripts, and on the other hand, it is said in the *Prajna Sutra*, "Wherever the prajna resides, buddhas of the ten directions always dwell. Therefore, if you wish to make offerings to the Buddha, you should make offerings to prajna because prajna is no different from the Buddha."

So once you have the *Diamond Cutter Sutra* with you, gods will always protect you from being harmed or disturbed by demons and heretics. Even if demons start to harm you, as long as you recite the *Diamond Cutter Sutra*, they would not dare to approach you.

For this reason, historically all the great masters of the Han Chinese region have placed great importance on the *Diamond Cutter Sutra*. One special example from the Tang dynasty is Chan Master Da Dian, who over the course of his life transcribed the *Diamond Sutra* 1,500 times and the *Lotus Sutra* thirty times.

Where There Is the *Diamond Cutter Sutra*, There Is the Buddha

"Where there is this sutra, there are buddhas and the most exalted disciples."

In the Tibetan edition this line was translated as: "Where there is this sutra, there are buddhas and lamas." It means that wherever prajna is, there is the Buddha and the spiritual teachers who guide sentient beings, so it is the genuine seat of enlightenment of the Buddha.

13. Upholding the Dharma

Then Subhuti asked the Buddha, "Bhagavan, what do you title this sutra? How should we take it into practice?"

Buddha told Subhuti, "This sutra is titled Vajra Prajna Paramita; with this title, you should uphold it."

BEFORE WE GET into the details, I want to remind you again that to study a sutra is not the same as to study a shastra or commentary. A commentary addresses only one issue at a time. But every sutra has its own unique attributes, and its content is like a pile of jewels without a relevant order. At one time, gold appears in front of you, beside it you might see silver, or sometimes coral. All kinds of jewels are piled together, and you can pick up any as you wish.

Commentaries composed by the great masters of history must summarize and assort these attributes and content in a teachable order. Likewise, when the Buddha gave the teaching on the *Diamond Cutter Sutra*, sometimes he talked about the merit of listening to this sutra, sometimes about the merit of paying respect to this sutra, and sometimes he dived into the content and examined closely the topic of emptiness that is conveyed in this sutra. When disciples compiled this sutra, they faithfully recorded the agenda and entire conversation, transcribing the questions and answers of the Buddha and Subhuti without altering the actual order.

Obviously, each question has its profound intended meaning and is aimed at a particular human tendency. For those who have strong attachment to their bodies, the Buddha asked, "Is a body the same size as Mount Meru, giant?" and then examined and concluded that bodies are empty in nature. For those who believe the world exists inherently, the Buddha asked, "Is the world broad?" and then destroyed their strong attachment to inherent existence. Therefore we should understand his questions were not aimless.

Earlier, it was said that this sutra is of immense merit. So here, Subhuti asks the Buddha how this sutra should be named, and in the future when we study and practice this sutra, what title should we use? Every word of the Buddha's answer delivers extraordinary meaning; not one word is irrelevant.

In this world, ordinary people often talk irresponsibly; in post-meditation periods, even arhats of the Basic Vehicle may occasionally say things that are not consistent with the Dharma and may even burst into laughter. This would never happen with the Buddha's discourse; each and every word uttered by the Buddha has intended meaning and is suitable for the capacity of the specific audience.

What did the Buddha answer? "This sutra is called *Vajra Prajna Paramita Sutra*; when transcribing or chanting this sutra in the future, you can use this title." The so-called vajra means the sutra can destroy everything yet cannot be damaged by anything. "Prajna" means wisdom. The *Sixth Patriarch Platform Sutra* says, "Prajna refers to wisdom in the Chinese language (Tang dynasty)." As for "paramita," it said, "This is Sanskrit; in the Chinese language, it means to reach the other shore." So "prajna paramita" has been translated as wisdom that has reached the other shore. The term can be explained in two ways: as for the wisdom of the path, it means one is approaching the wisdom of the Buddha; for the wisdom of fruition, it means one has already attained the wisdom of the Buddha.

According to the *Commentary on the Ornament of Clear Realization*, prajna falls into four categories: prajna of words, prajna of its nature, prajna of the path, and prajna of the fruition. Basing his understanding on Dignaga's "Wisdom is nondual, path and words are just named," Koringpa of the Sakyapa categorized prajna into prajna of words, prajna of the path, and prajna of fruition. The ultimate other shore is the prajna of fruition that is the wisdom of the buddha, which is the theme of the *Diamond Cutter Sutra*. Therefore when we recite, transcribe, or meditate on the sutra, we should keep this in mind.

EMPTINESS IS NOT NOTHINGNESS

"Why? Subhuti, the Buddha said prajna paramita is not prajna paramita."

The buddhas of the three times have all taught prajna paramita. However, the prajna paramita in sutras can only guide sentient beings temporarily. Heretics and non-Buddhists have no interest in studying prajna paramita; some Buddhist followers are fortunate enough to listen to it, but they are frightened by emptiness; and some Buddhists have been practicing the emptiness of prajna, but since their virtuous roots are not mature, they cannot perceive the way things really are. In order to benefit these sentient beings, the Buddha has spent a great deal of time explaining prajna paramita.

However, this perception only appears before ordinary sentient beings who perceive delusively. If examined closely, prajna paramita is also empty by nature, free from any characteristics. As said in the *Avatamsaka Sutra*, "The nature is pure, free from contamination or confusion." At the ultimate level, prajna paramita is not prajna paramita, so there is no difference between "reaching the other shore" and "having not yet reached the other shore." However, within the conventional, appearances arising from causes and conditions never cease, so it can be called prajna paramita.

Why is it necessary for the Buddha to explain every phenomenon this way? The purpose is to guide all sentient beings to realize emptiness and attain the state of prajna paramita. Obviously, emptiness is not nothingness. Rather, emptiness is nothing other than appearance; these two aspects are indivisible, they are not two separate things. Even after the Buddha reached buddhahood, he did not do nothing; instead, he appeared turning the wheel of Dharma, and he entered parinirvana and so forth.

"Subhuti, what do you think? Has the Tathagata taught any Dharma?"
Subhuti replied, "Bhagavan, the Tathagata has nothing to teach."

Earlier, we examined the idea that the Tathagata has never taught any Dharma. This topic is revisited here because the emptiness of prajna is closely related to the Buddha's second turning of the wheel of Dharma of non-characteristics. Since all phenomena are empty by nature, does it mean the second turning of the wheel of Dharma that reveals emptiness also does not exist?

Subhuti completely understood the intended meaning of the Buddha. He knew that turning the wheel of Dharma does appear within the conventional, but in ultimate reality, from the moment he reached buddhahood until he entered parinirvana, the Tathagata has never said one word or uttered one sentence. As it is said in the sutra, "Since I became the Tathagata, I have never uttered one word of the Dharma."

Therefore, in the ultimate reality, the Dharma taught by the Tathagata has no form, no shape, and no reference point, so if we cling to it with conceptual thoughts, we will miss the ultimate meaning. However, in order to guide sentient beings of different capacities, the Buddha gave a variety of Dharma teachings according to their disposition. This can be admitted within the conventional.

When Will Contradictory Entities Coexist?

Again, the Buddha examined the empty nature of all phenomena by distinguishing the difference between particles and worlds.

"Subhuti, what do you think? Are the particles of the three-thousandfold universe numerous?"

Subhuti said, "Countless, Bhagavan."

"Subhuti, the Tathagata said particles are not particles so they are called 'particles.'"

People unfamiliar with the ultimate truth and the conventional truth may find this part difficult to understand. What on earth does the Buddha mean? Isn't it contradictory to say that since they are not particles, they are particles? Just as some people have no understanding of the idea that "form is emptiness, emptiness is form," they believe it is impossible for two contradictory states or entities to coexist. However, once you have mastered the idea of dependent origination, apparent contradictions are not an issue at all.

As we all know, within the conventional, we can say that a mud pie is composed of countless particles, so the particles that constitute the three-thousandfold universe must be even more countless. On this occasion

Subhuti appeared to be a little slow, not quite understanding the intended meaning of the Buddha when he responded with "countless," as if he had a great attachment to particles. Because of this misunderstanding, the Buddha began to examine the particles and concluded that they are empty by nature. At that time the Buddha said, "Although it appears there are so many particles, through the approaches to ultimate analysis, all these particles are not particles."

Why did he say this? When we studied the wisdom chapter of *Guide to the Bodhisattva's Way of Life*, we examined and concluded that particles, whether indivisible or divisible, do not truly exist. Regarding indivisible particles, when they make up bigger particles or some substance, if there is a particle to the east of the center particle, the center particle must have a part facing east, which means this indivisible particle has different parts. If this is the case, how can there be even the smallest indivisible particles?

As *The Four Hundred Stanzas on the Middle Way* says, "If a particle can relate to the east, it must have a part facing east, and if the smallest particle has different parts, it can be divided, so how can it be the smallest indivisible particle?" If they are divisible particles, they can be divided continuously, so they are not unchanging, inherent particles. Through such examination on the ultimate level, it is even untenable to say that there is dust on the Buddha statue, or that one's clothes are dirty.

If particles exist inherently, then by whatever method is used to examine them, their inherent existence would not be refuted; but we have seen that this conclusion is impossible. Although particles do appear before the deluded eyes of sentient beings, and when dust falls into our eyes we feel pain, yet with close examination and in the ultimate analysis, these particles are not particles at all.

This World System Is Also Like Dreams and Illusions

The Tathagata said that since world systems are not world systems, they are called "world systems."

As the *Avatamsaka Sutra* says, the three-thousandfold universe has come into being through illusory causes and conditions; under scrutiny, how can such a real universe exist? The King of Aspiration Prayer: Samantabhadra's

"Aspiration to Good Actions" also says, "There are universes as many as the number of particles in every single particle." Just think, how can all the numerous universes squeeze into one particle if they exist intrinsically?

Of course, to sentient beings with delusive perception, it might appear that this world has over seven billion people, and in a wider spectrum, there are also extraterrestrial universes. However, with ultimate analysis, these universes do not exist at all.

The connotations to any topic of the *Diamond Cutter Sutra* are fathomless. Each topic requires understanding and comparison on two levels. Regarding the existence of phenomena: as conventional phenomena, they exist absolutely, but when examined at the ultimate level, phenomena are as insubstantial as dreams and illusions. Make sure you have mastered this key point!

A MAN WITH A PURE HEART SEES EVERYTHING AS A BUDDHA; A MAN WITH AN IMPURE HEART SEES ONLY UNPLEASANT OBJECTS

"Subhuti, what do you think? Can the Tathagata be met by the thirty-two excellent marks?"

"No, Bhagavan. The Tathagata cannot be met by the thirty-two excellent marks. Why? The Tathagata said, the thirty-two marks are not thirty-two marks so are called 'the thirty-two marks.'"

Due to habitual tendencies from beginningless time, sentient beings perceive the same object quite differently. Generally speaking, ordinary people can see only the impure five aggregates, whereas bodhisattvas always perceive pure noble beings. Therefore some people have attachment toward the appearance of the Tathagata because they believe that samsara is impure, whereas the ten powers, four fearlessnesses, eighteen extraordinary attributes, thirty-two major excellent marks, and eighty minor excellent marks signify greatness, and only the latter is worthy of pursuing.[6]

This thinking is even reasonable according to the standards of conventional pure cognition because in the conventional sense, purity and impurity are indeed different. For example, the teachers of the heretics saw that Buddha Shakyamuni had eighteen types of ugly marks, whereas Venerable Kashyapa saw that the Buddha had thirty-two major excellent marks and eighty minor excellent marks. Therefore, conventionally, people with pure hearts see the Buddha with major and minor marks, whereas those who have impure hearts can only perceive various ugly marks.[7]

Many people believe, "The major and minor marks adorning the Buddha are real even in the definitive meaning, nothing could be more supreme than this, and the thirty-two excellent marks would never be empty." Such pure cognition turns out to be unreasonable when analyzed at the ultimate level. In order to refute this notion, the Buddha asked Subhuti, "Can we meet the essence of the Buddha by his perfect form body with excellent marks?" Subhuti's capacity is beyond ordinary; having realized the nature of buddhas and sentient beings, he replied: "It is unreasonable to meet the Buddha by his excellent marks."

Why did he say this? Because the thirty-two excellent marks are the excellent qualities of the form body, or rupakaya (form body falls into sambhogakaya and nirmanakaya, and Buddha Shakyamuni is a supreme form of nirmanakaya, or emanation). It is impossible to meet the Tathagata through the thirty-two physical excellent marks, which are only dream-like illusions appearing in front of bodhisattvas and ordinary people. Buddhist sutras with definitive meaning would never admit they exist inherently.

The ultimate form body is actually the dharmakaya, or truth body, which does not have any excellent marks. Just as said in the *Avatamsaka Sutra*, "The dharmakaya of buddhas is inconceivable—no form, no shape, and no appearance at all."

In general, at the conventional level, buddhas have the thirty-two excellent marks, while at the ultimate level, the nature of the form body is the truth body, which does not appear physically. In some commentaries, form body and truth body are explained as completely separate entities. This is not correct.

RECITING THE *DIAMOND CUTTER SUTRA* WHOLEHEARTEDLY CAN UPROOT SELF-CLINGING AND SEVER CONCEPTUAL THOUGHTS

"Subhuti, if there is a son or daughter of noble qualities who gives away as many bodies as the sand grains in the Ganges River, and if there is a person who upholds and explains this sutra to other people, or even just a four-line verse, the latter creates more merit than the former."

"Giving away the seven jewels filling up the entire three-thousandfold universe" has been mentioned twice before. Here it is "giving away as many bodies as the sand grains in the Ganges River." The former is an ordinary material offering; the latter is infinite generosity (body offering) because its merit is unimaginable. However, it is still far inferior to a Dharma offering. So this root text shows both the supremeness of a Dharma offering and the immense merit of upholding the *Diamond Cutter Sutra*.

A story in the *Sutra of the Wise and Foolish* goes like this. Once upon a time, the Bhagavan was born as the King Moon Light who was very kind and charitable. Knowing this, a Brahmin went to see him and said, "Giving away external material things does not create the greatest merit, only infinite generosity can perfect your merit, so you should give your body to me." King Moon Light acceded to his request, and before he gave away his body under a tree in the Deer Park, he said, "I have given away my body under this tree 999 times already, adding this time, it will be exactly 1,000 times total." As we see, in order to benefit sentient beings, bodhisattvas take great pains and endure great hardship to practice the perfection of generosity over the course of many years.

As we all know, the merit of a body offering is immense, but here the Buddha says that even if you gave away as many bodies as there are sand grains in the Ganges River, it would not match the merit of upholding just a four-line verse of the *Diamond Cutter Sutra*.

Basically, upholding is of two kinds: ostensible upholding and authentic upholding. Ostensible upholding means to appear reciting, "All the conditioned phenomena are like dreams, illusions, water bubbles, and reflections . . ." with the text in one's hands, but have a bee in one's bonnet, doubting and suspecting all the time. With such upholding, it is impossible to surpass the merit of body offering in hundreds of thousands of eons. Only authentic upholding—that is, mastering the most profound and definitive meaning of the sutra and explaining to other people—can create great merit, as said in this passage.

The Sixth Patriarch also remarked, "Reciting the *Diamond Cutter Sutra* wholeheartedly can uproot self-clinging and sever conceptual thoughts." Only through attentively chanting the *Diamond Cutter Sutra* and gaining certainty about the meaning of the sutra are we able to uproot the attachment toward persons and the attachment toward phenomena, as well as various conceptual thoughts, to reach enlightenment. Therefore only by chanting it in such a way can the merit exceed that of giving away one's body.

The Bhagavan intended to inspire sentient beings' interests so that they could be introduced to the *Diamond Cutter Sutra*. For those who know nothing about Buddhism, in order to verify the capacity of beings, we can first tell them that just chanting the *Diamond Cutter Sutra* one time could create immense merit; then, when they start to form some idea of the sutra, we can explain further that chanting it absent-mindedly is not good, that we should master its meaning, give rise to reasonable thoughts, and give up chanting it in a careless manner.

Upholding

Upholding can be understood in two ways: completely understanding the meaning of the sutra and constantly recollecting the contents of the sutra. Merely chanting it with lip movement will not create much merit, so we must master its ultimate meaning.

In the Tibetan edition, "upholding" has been translated as "upholding, mastering, transcribing, and contemplating accordingly." Contemplating accordingly is the foremost endeavor. Nowadays, a great many people have been chanting the *Diamond Cutter Sutra* regularly, but very few contemplate it accordingly. If you do not understand what the sutra actually says, how can it be called "upholding" the sutra? The *Diamond Cutter Sutra* has immense merit, so if we only chant it absent-mindedly without understanding the deeper connotations of the words, we are not likely to attain such merit. Therefore we should master its genuine meaning according to scriptures and logic!

14. Peace Free of Conceptions

GREAT COMPASSION CAN ARISE ONLY WITH THE WISDOM OF EMPTINESS

Then, after hearing this sutra, Subhuti deeply understood the intended meaning and burst into tears. While weeping, he said to the Buddha, "Oh, so wondrous, Bhagavan."

Burst into tears

THE PHRASE "burst into tears" explains the perspective of emptiness. After the Buddha taught the ultimate merit of this sutra, Subhuti sincerely realized its incomparable supremeness and from the depth of his heart felt overwhelming joy.

As described in *The Introduction to the Middle Way*, "Upon hearing the teachings on emptiness, if great joy rises again and again, and from such great joy, a person bursts into tears and their hair stands up on end, this kind of person must have the capacity to receive the teachings on emptiness." Therefore, according to this passage, Subhuti completely met the criterion for understanding the ultimate meaning of emptiness.

Weeping

Weeping describes the aspect of great compassion. After perceiving the supremeness of emptiness, Subhuti had the thought that numerous sentient beings in the three realms of cyclic existence have no chance to hear this teaching, and such unbearable great compassion arose in his being that he could not help weeping. As said in the sutra, "Great compassion is the root of all bodhisattvas; great compassion is the mother of all wisdom."

Wondrous

In the Tibetan edition, the word "wondrous" appears twice. In Xuan Zang's Chinese translation, it is, "So wondrous, Bhagavan! Most wondrous,

Sugata!" The exclamation is also repeated. Why did Subhuti call it "wondrous"? Because, relying on emptiness, virtuous roots can be implanted in the hearts of ordinary beings, their illusions can be eradicated, and rebirth into cyclic existence can be severed. Such excellence cannot be found in ordinary teachings.

WHY IS THE *DIAMOND CUTTER SUTRA* SO WONDROUS?

"The Buddha has explained a profound sutra. Such a sutra I have never heard the likes of since I acquired the eyes of wisdom."

Subhuti is a great arhat who acquired the eyes of wisdom when he first attained sotapanna, or the fruition of stream-entry. The conventional eyes of ordinary people can perceive only form or physical phenomena, whereas the wisdom eyes of arhats can see everything and can read the minds of sentient beings and hear any sound. Of course, as arhats of the Basic Vehicle, they have not yet thoroughly mastered emptiness, and their wisdom cannot compare with that of the bodhisattvas of the Great Vehicle. As the sutra says, "The emptiness realized by listeners, or shravakas, is like the water that pools in a footprint of an ox, whereas the emptiness realized by bodhisattvas is like the water in great oceans." As we can see, although shravakas, or listeners, have realized emptiness, their level of realization is not very high.

The *Diamond Cutter Sutra* can eliminate doubts and attachment toward "existence" and "nonexistence." It can also reveal the truth that all phenomena do not inherently exist. Therefore it has immense merit. Such a supreme doctrine cannot be found in the scriptures of the Basic Vehicle. This might be the first time that Subhuti encountered the sutra, so he felt it to be extremely wondrous.

I myself have great faith in the *Diamond Cutter Sutra* and also agree that this sutra is extraordinary. The great masters who have spread this sutra are indeed marvelous! Believers who have studied, upheld, and chanted this sutra are also marvelous!

With Faith, Realizing Emptiness Is Possible

"Bhagavan, if after listening to this sutra some people gain pure faith and finally realize the way things are, we should understand that such people have attained the most wondrous merit."

When we gain some worldly achievement, such as fame, profit, or support, it is not marvelous because a great number of ordinary people can do the same. However, if we gain pure faith in the merit of the *Diamond Cutter Sutra* and realize the wisdom of the ultimate reality, then it is the most marvelous merit.

Pure faith

What is pure faith? Believing the *Diamond Cutter Sutra* is marvelous, a supreme teaching taught by the Buddha. What is impure faith? Seeming to believe the *Diamond Cutter Sutra* is supreme but suspecting its merit might not be so immense. Such faith has been blemished by doubts, so it is impure.

Whoever gains pure faith in the *Diamond Cutter Sutra* would certainly attain the wisdom of ultimate reality, the most definitive and thorough enlightenment. As said by Bodhisattva Maitreya, "Faith is the source of the path and the mother of merit." Although some people believe undertaking a big project or construction plan is extraordinary, it is in fact not very amazing; others may think it is marvelous to have the power of clairvoyance, but so do heretics, ghosts, and demons, so it is not worth admiring. However, if you realize the ultimate reality through faith in the *Diamond Cutter Sutra*, as the Sixth Patriarch did, it is the most wondrous of all the most wondrous feats in the world!

No Attachment to Existence, Still Less to Nonexistence

"Bhagavan, ultimate reality is free from characteristics, so the Tathagata said it is called 'ultimate reality.'"

In the Tibetan edition, before this line, there is the question, "Why is that?" to connect this response to the previous assertion. So this entire line carries the meaning: Why is it most marvelous to perceive the nature of ultimate reality? Because ultimate reality is actually free from characteristics.

The reason why ordinary people cannot reach liberation is because they attach to characteristics, either "existence" or "nonexistence." Therefore they are tethered by desire, hatred, and ignorance. However, noble beings transcend this state; they do not have any kind of attachment and have perceived the nature of ultimate reality free from all mental fabrication.

How, then, to reach the state of ultimate reality? In the "Wisdom" chapter of *Guide to the Bodhisattva's Way of Life*, it says first meditate for a long time that all phenomena lack true existence, so that the habitual tendency of holding on to the inherent existence of all phenomena can be eliminated, then apply this meditation to the remedy itself—that is, understand that the concept of "lacking existence" itself lacks true existence—and in this way our subtle attachment toward emptiness itself will also be eradicated. If these two steps have been successfully applied in practice, one can finally reach the state described in *Guide to the Bodhisattva's Way of Life*: "Once neither a thing or non-thing remains before the mind, then as there is no other [alternative] . . . [finally the mind that] apprehends [objects] will cease and be totally pacified" (chapter 9, verse 34).

In general, when examining the meaning of ultimate reality, no characteristics, form, or shape are findable. In sutras with definitive meaning, the Buddha also said that at the ultimate level, there are no truly existent characteristics. The so-called characteristics are only provisionally established in the illusory conventional reality for convenience, because the Tathagata has never said there has been any truly existing entity.

WHEN DARKNESS EXISTS IN ONE PLACE, LIGHT MUST EXIST SOMEWHERE ELSE

"Bhagavan, now that I have listened to this sutra, it is not difficult for me to gain faith and uphold it. However, in the future, in the last five hundred years, if some sentient beings encounter this sutra, listen to, gain faith in, and uphold it, these people would indeed be most wondrous."

Why did he say this? Because when the Buddha was in this world, it was the "phase of fruition"—Buddhism was flourishing and it was quite common to reach enlightenment, arhathood, or bodhisattvahood. Both the time and sentient beings' capacity were superior to ours, so it was not so difficult to gain faith in and uphold the sutra.

Earlier Subhuti said he had never heard such supreme teachings before attaining the eyes of wisdom, so realizing emptiness was extremely wondrous, but now after second thought, he said, "It is not that wondrous; right now Buddhism is flourishing, plus I am number one in teaching emptiness, so it should not be considered difficult for me to gain faith and uphold such a teaching of emptiness."

According to Kamalashila, the emptiness realized by listeners, or shravakas, is only a partial realization and not complete, so Subhuti said, "Through listening to this sutra, I have realized emptiness, but the state of my realization is not high enough, therefore it is not that wondrous. However, in the future, when great bodhisattvas realize the perfect emptiness through the *Diamond Cutter Sutra*, it will be the most wondrous realization of all." This passage also indirectly distinguishes the emptiness realized by shravakas and bodhisattvas; the former is limited and partial and the latter is infinite and complete.

In Chan Buddhism, the terms "comprehended realization" and "enlightened realization" have been commonly used. What Subhuti attained on that first occasion was comprehended realization, a thorough comprehension of emptiness in the Great Vehicle, but not direct perceiving. However, in the future, bodhisattvas of the Great Vehicle have the chance to attain complete and perfect enlightenment on emptiness.

In the future, in the last five hundred years
This concept, which is widely accepted in both Han Chinese regions and in Tibet, has been explained earlier. Some people believe that when the Buddha lived in this world Buddhism flourished, as it did in the five hundred years after his parinirvana, but after that five hundred years we entered the time of degeneration. "The five hundred years of the time of degeneration" does not necessarily mean only one period of five hundred years but could be multiple five hundred years, one after another.

Some doctrines say that Buddhism undergoes both a flourishing period and a disappearing period, whereas scriptures with definitive meaning tell us the Buddhadharma would never disappear. In Vajrayana, as the *Kalachakra*, the *Wheel of Time*, says, "The so-called time of degeneration means that after the Buddhadharma disappears in one place, it will flourish in another place, just as when sunlight disappears from one part of the earth it must shine on another part of the earth."

It also says in the *Inconceivable Sutra* of the Sutrayana, "The Buddha has never entered parinirvana. The Dharma will always remain in the world." Therefore the so-called five hundred years of the time of degeneration is only a manifestation before some sentient beings.

As we have learned, it was not so rare to listen to the *Diamond Cutter Sutra* when the Buddha lived in the world. However, in our time, when the five degenerations are rampant, it is indeed wondrous that we can listen to this teaching and savor the inconceivable taste of emptiness!

Nagarjuna also remarked, "After understanding that emptiness pervades all phenomena, we should know that all karmic effects arise dependently. So it [Dharma] is the rarest of the most rare, the most wondrous of the most wondrous."

Some people might disagree because they believe that it is wondrous to make a fortune, attain a high social status, and gain enormous prestige. In fact, these things are all trivial. What is really marvelous in such an inferior time of degeneration when the Buddha has entered parinirvana for years and people who authentically practice Buddhadharma are decreasing? What is truly marvelous is that through the blessing of gurus and the Three Jewels, we get the chance to listen to the teaching on emptiness, savor the supreme taste of the inconceivable ambrosia of the Buddhadharma, and attain the wisdom of emptiness that frees us from cyclic existence. This is indeed the most wondrous of the most wondrous.

WHY CAN'T WE SHAKE OFF AFFLICTIVE EMOTIONS?

"Why? This person would not have any conception of a self, a person, a sentient being, and a living being."

Freedom from all conceptions is of course the highest state. Sentient beings in the three realms of cyclic existence always fail to shake off afflictive emotions. The reason for their failure is their four conceptions. If these four conceptions were severed, beings would be free from all sufferings. Therefore, in regard to the teaching on emptiness, the more you listen and the more you practice, the greater your benefit.

Some people can cut off self-clinging right away. Others may not be able to do it immediately, but with time their self-clinging lessens day by day until it completely disappears. Then its disappearance is the most wondrous in the world.

As mentioned earlier, attachment to self is called the "conception of a self." Attachment to others is called the "conception of a person"—for example, thinking, "These are people in our Buddhist institute," or "We are Sichuan people," or "How can human beings survive?" Attachment to sentient beings is called "conception of a sentient being"—for example, thinking, "How many sentient beings are there in the three-thousandfold universe?" Attachment to the longevity of self and other is called the "conception of a living being"—for instance, most people are afraid of death, so they are very attentive when we hold the Dharma Gathering of Buddha Amitayus; before the last day, when we usually collect the number of mantra repetitions from each participant, some of them have finished one hundred thousand repetitions.

If we realize emptiness, these four conceptions would be gone. Master Han Shan has said it well in the *Vajra Destroying All Doubts*: "The four conceptions are suchness by nature; once you realize this, you realize the dharmakaya. Therefore it is said that when you are free from all the conceptions, you can be called 'the Buddha.' This is so wondrous."

WHEN YOU SEE CHARACTERISTICS FREE FROM CHARACTERISTICS, YOU HAVE REALIZED THE NATURE OF ULTIMATE REALITY

"Why? Since the conception of a self is free from characteristics, so are the conceptions of a person, a sentient being, and a living being."

Through examining the selflessness of people and the selflessness of phenomena, the conception of a self would not have the chance to exist. When the conception of a self is negated, the other three conceptions also cannot be established. Of course, this is examination at the ultimate level. At the relative level, the conception of a self, a person, a sentient being, and a living being can all be fabricated.

The *Lankavatara Sutra* says, "All phenomena arise within the conventional, yet they arise from selflessness." It means that any phenomenon we can hear or see belongs to the conventional perspective. From the ultimate view, there are no such characteristics at all.

Once we know that the conception of a self does not exist through reasoning, we can conclude further that the conception of a person and a sentient being do not exist either. This is because if you are able to see one thing is emptiness, you can see everything is emptiness. If the conception of a person and a sentient being do not exist, how can the conception of a living being exist? Therefore, in the ultimate meaning, the four conceptions do not exist. This is a realization of the ultimate reality.

The Sixth Patriarch said, "When the four conceptions are eliminated, it is the nature of ultimate reality, the heart of the Buddha (Buddha's wisdom)." The Sixth Patriarch is a great accomplisher. His remarks are very concise, but they are of immense blessing and unique inspiration. By listening and practicing this teaching of transcendental wisdom, such great realization can also arise in our being.

THE REAL BUDDHA IS ONE'S OWN MIND

"Why? Transcending conceptions is called 'the Buddhas.'"

The nature of all phenomena is free from these four conceptions, and the Buddha is free from the four conceptions. Obviously, before the illusory appearance of sentient beings, Buddha Shakyamuni has his characteristics and form, and gurus also have their characteristics and form. Some people look for a guru everywhere, but actually the genuine guru is one's own mind. Attachment to characteristics won't make you enlightened; the genuine Buddha is only in transcending the fabricated conceptions of "existence" and "nonexistence." Vasubandhu also said, "The Tathagata is free from any conceptions. We followers should emulate this."

A story in Chinese Chan tradition can illuminate this idea. Once, in a monastery, a very young novice monk urinated in front of a buddha statue in a shrine room. Upon seeing this, an old monk berated him, "This world is so big, why do you have to piss in front of the Buddha?" The little monk replied, "The ten directions and the three times, east and west, south and north, left and right, above and below, buddhas are everywhere, and even a single particle holds buddhas as many as the number of particles! You tell me, where should I pee?" Speechless, the old monk uttered no word.

Once when the Tibetan Master Gendun Chophel visited Lhasa, a group of geshes wanted to debate with him. After learning their intention, he deliberately brought a buddha statue before them and knocked it with his smoking pipe. Offended, the geshes said, "You showed no respect to the Buddha; you have broken the precepts of taking refuge." The master refuted, "All phenomena are free from characteristics. Where is the Buddha then?"

This triggered a fierce debate between them, and finally the geshes lost. They had to tell people on the street, "We have studied debating for over twenty years, but today we have been defeated by this old man. We have to admit that there is no fault to knock a smoking pipe on a buddha statue and, moreover, we have to accept that this act can create merit!" Therefore, in the nature of ultimate reality, there is no single characteristic that truly exists.

The Fundamental Wisdom of the Middle Way also says that the Tathagata has transcended all mental fabrication, while ordinary people always cling to characteristics. In fact the nature of ultimate reality is the nature of mind, which is free from mental fabrication. This is the secret meaning of the Buddha.

To our eyes, gurus have their conventional characteristics, but in fact gurus are just our own mind. Similarly, the Buddha is our mind—our mind is free from mental fabrication, and freedom from mental fabrication is the nature of phenomena. Whenever we realize this, we see the Buddha indeed!

THOSE WHO HAVE ENCOUNTERED THE TEACHING OF EMPTINESS HAVE GREAT MERIT

The Buddha said to Subhuti, "Thus it is. Thus it is. After hearing this sutra, if someone is not frightened, not terrified, not fearful, this person is most wondrous."

The Buddha was very satisfied with Subhuti's realization of emptiness. Meanwhile, he prophesied that in the future, particularly the five hundred years of the time of degeneration, if through the fortunate causes and conditions of past lives someone receives the teachings on emptiness of transcendental wisdom before qualified teachers of the Great Vehicle and does not get frightened when hearing of the selflessness of people, does not get terrified when hearing of the selflessness of phenomena, and does not get fearful when hearing of the selflessness of both people and phenomena, this person and his like are indeed marvelous.

From Kamalashila's point of view, "not frightened" is the aspect of listening, "not terrified" is the perspective of reflecting, and "not fearful" is in regard to meditating. Such people must have accumulated merit before countless buddhas. In this life their virtuous condition and virtuous root ripen, so they have the supreme causes and conditions to receive teachings on ultimate reality without fear.

People with the capacity to comprehend the Great Vehicle would have no fear after hearing the teachings on emptiness. Apparently fear here does not mean the same fear ordinary people have toward ghosts or vicious people, but rather not being able to accept the emptiness theory of the Great Vehicle, thinking it is unreasonable.

In the past when I visited Thailand, before a presentation, a master kindly reminded me that it would be better to avoid talking about the Middle Way or emptiness, otherwise some people in the audience might give rise to negative views. Therefore I was very discreet during the entire talk; every time emptiness was about to be touched on, I immediately held my tongue and switched to other topics. However, at the end of my talk, questions on emptiness were raised by the audience, so I still had to address the topic. But at least, from what the master suggested, we can conclude there are some people who can accept emptiness only from the standpoint of the Basic Vehicle.

Generally speaking, intelligent people would not be terrified by emptiness, nor would people who have never been exposed to emptiness be fearful, but people in between those two—that is, less intelligent people who have heard about emptiness—would be scared. As said in *The Four Hundred Stanzas on the Middle Way*, "People who have not heard (about emptiness) would not be fearful, the omniscient would not either; only those who have insufficient understanding of it would be fearful."

Once in the past, two practitioners with immaculate precepts paid a visit to Venerable Atisha. At first, the master taught them the theory of selflessness from the view of the Basic Vehicle. They were overjoyed. But when the master began to explain transcendental wisdom in the Great Vehicle, they were terrified and beseeched him to immediately stop. When hearing the master chanting the *Heart Sutra*, their fear became so unbearable that they ran away with their hands covering their ears. As we can imagine, very few people who have not entered the Great Vehicle path would not be frightened by its teachings on emptiness.

Nowadays, all sorts of wrong views are thriving. We are so fortunate to meet with the teachings on emptiness. Nevertheless, the wisdom of emptiness in the mindstream of ordinary beings is still very weak. It might arise a couple of times, or for a short while, but if we don't familiarize ourselves with the teachings or contemplate emptiness for a couple of months straight, our small wisdom of mindfulness would soon be obscured by conceptual thoughts and would gradually "dissolve into the basic space (dharmadhatu)." In order to strengthen this right view, we should spend more time reading books on the Middle Way and emptiness.

RECORDS IN SUTRAS ARE LIKE A CHATTING HISTORY

"Why is that? Subhuti, the Tathagata has said the highest perfection is not the highest perfection, so it is the highest perfection."

In this world, no matter if it is the six perfections or the ten perfections, the most supreme is non-perfection, for non-perfection is indescribable with words or thoughts. Non-perfection is not ordinary mundane theory, but rather the ultimate wisdom free from any mental fabrication. For this reason, the Buddha said it is the highest perfection.

The translations by Yi Jing and Xuan Zang as well as the Tibetan edition are not much different in their phrasing of this statement. They all say, as one of the translations has it, "Prajnaparamita (the perfection of transcendental wisdom) has been said to be the most supreme, not only by me (Buddha Shakyamuni) but also by countless buddhas of the past who have said with one voice that it is the most supreme perfection."

Why is that? Because prajnaparamita is the secret meaning of all the buddhas. As *Guide to the Bodhisattva's Way of Life* says:

> All of these practices were taught
> by the Mighty One for the sake of wisdom.
> Therefore those who wish to pacify suffering
> should generate this wisdom.

The other five perfections of generosity, discipline, and so forth have all been elaborated by the Buddha for the sake of the perfection of wisdom. The perfection of wisdom is foremost, it is the ultimate of all phenomena.

Although such perfection does not inherently exist at the ultimate level, within the conventional, all the buddhas and bodhisattvas have said that the perfection of wisdom is the most supreme and the highest among all the perfections.

As mentioned earlier, Buddhist sutras are not as clearly arranged as are commentaries. For instance, *The Introduction to the Middle Way* first explains the state of the first bhumi of bodhisattvas, and then goes to the state of the second bhumi, and so on. The commentary is explicit and in good order.

Buddhist sutras take a different style. The contents are recorded more like a colloquial history of who said this and who said that. And the topic of the chat could always be switched without a hint beforehand. When the perfection of generosity has been explained, the perfection of patience might pop up in the next sentence. As soon as you have adjusted to reading about the perfection of patience, the perfection of generosity is back. You should keep this in mind and get accustomed to it.

Now let's move on to the perfection of patience.

WHAT IS THE HIGHEST LEVEL OF PATIENCE?

"Subhuti, the perfection of patience, the Tathagata said, is not the perfection of patience."

In *White Lotus: The Great Biography of Buddha Shakyamuni*, we read that the Buddha underwent numerous hardships for practicing patience on the path at his causal stage, meaning the period of time the Buddha was accumulating merit and wisdom before he attained his goal.[8] However, when scrutinizing this passage with wisdom, we find that there is no person who practices patience, nor are there objects for practicing patience nor methods for practicing patience.

Apparently in the illusory appearance of sentient beings, the Buddha did cut out flesh from his own body and did give it to sentient beings, and within the conventional we can call it a form of patience and tolerance. However, at the ultimate level there is no patience, and this is actually the most supreme method to practicing patience.

As practitioners following the way of bodhisattvas, we should master the original meaning of "emptiness of the three spheres," for only when we realize emptiness can we tolerate all forms of suffering. Otherwise, when our seats are taken, when our cottages are torn down, it would easily kindle hatred—which means you have no view on emptiness and you have not reached the perfection of patience. Think about how the Buddha practiced patience at his causal stage. And then look at us, how easily we get annoyed and even get into fights over trivia.

Then there are people who believe they have reached a high level of realization and always brag about their realization, but when they encounter the tiniest unfavorable condition or are in conflict with other people, their hatred is at an extremely high level indeed, and their so-called realization is completely uncovered as a delusion.

In Tibet there is a kind of red worm that little kids like to tease by rolling them back and forth on the ground in the sun. The worms get pissed off and in short order their bodies puff up, and puff up—until they explode. Are there people in your life like this kind of worm, who burst with rage at the least bit of irritation?

How Did the Buddha Practice Patience?

"Why? Subhuti, when I was chopped up by King Kali in the past, I didn't have the conception of a self, a person, a sentient being, or a living being."

When the Buddha was born as the Sage Forbearance, there was a king called Kali who was extremely brutal and unprincipled. One day, he and his queen and concubines went to hunt in a wood. As he paused to rest in a garden, his queen and concubines went to pick flowers in the depth of the woods, where they blundered into a sage who was meditating. They all gained faith in this sage and sat around him to request a teaching. Out of compassion and in order to eliminate their attachment and lust, the sage accepted their request and began to teach them the Dharma.

Upon awakening, the king did not see any of his women and started to search for them. Finally, he found they were all sitting around the sage. He roared with rage, "Who are you?"

The sage answered calmly, "I am the Sage Forbearance."

"Why are you with my queens?"

The sage said, "My mind is pure and free from stains."

The king pumped him, "If you are free from stains, have you attained arhatship?"

"No."

"Have you become a non-returner (anagami), a once-returner (sakadagami), a stream-enterer (sotapanna)?"

With modesty, the sage said, "None of them."

The king blustered, "Since you have not achieved any of the noble attainments, who would believe that nothing happened among you guys? Say, what on earth are you doing here?"

With honesty, the sage answered, "I am here practicing patience."

Unsheathing his sword, the king howled, "Let me test your practice on patience." Then the king chopped off the hands, feet, . . . of the sage. All the while, the sage had not even a moment of ill will toward the king.

Having witnessed his violence, the gods were irritated and showered sand rain from the sky. Seeing this, the king was frightened. Kneeling down, he confessed before the sage, who compassionately responded with this aspiration: "When I reach buddhahood in the future, I will come to liberate you first."

Afterward, when the gods asked the Sage Forbearance if he regretted what had happened, he said not a bit, and through the power of his true words, his body was completely restored.

When Buddha Shakyamuni was enlightened, there were five monks who were taught by him at the very start. Among them, Venerable Kaundinya was reborn from King Kali.

WITH GREAT WISDOM, ONE CAN ERADICATE HATRED

The next line explains why the Buddha's mind is pure.

"Why is that? When my body was segmented, if I had the conceptions of a self, a person, a sentient being, or a living being, I must have hatred."

The Compendium of Valid Cognition says that with the notion of "self" or "I" the conception of "other" is bound to arise; and with the clinging to self and other, desire and anger naturally arise, leading to various afflictive emotions and faults.

When the Buddha was Sage Forbearance, if he had had the four conceptions, he would definitely have harbored aversion toward King Kali. But he didn't. So as we can see, he must have had the wisdom of emptiness. Therefore it is of foremost importance to listen, reflect, and meditate on the teachings of emptiness. If we are not imbued with emptiness, the afflictive emotions—desire, anger, and so forth—of ordinary people cannot be suppressed or avoided, and when they arise they gnaw at us. However, once we are equipped with the wisdom of emptiness, afflictive emotions will immediately disappear without a trace.

STOP PAYING MERE LIP SERVICE WHEN PRACTICING PATIENCE

"Subhuti, I can also recall that when I was born as Sage Forbearance for five hundred lifetimes, I had no conceptions of a self, a person, a sentient being, or a living being."

His Holiness Jigme Phuntsok Rinpoche taught us *White Lotus: The Great Biography of Buddha Shakyamuni.* Every time it came to the Buddha's practice on patience and tolerance toward enemies, and hardship during Dharma practice, and giving up his bodies and lives, His Holiness would choke with sobs and tears. Unfortunately, we did not have simultaneous translation at that time. Sometimes His Holiness cried for a long time, but the Chinese sangha members didn't know what was going on and had to wait until I translated these passages for them the next morning.

When Buddha Shakyamuni was born as the Sage Forbearance for five hundred lifetimes, in each life he had no conception of a self, a person, a sentient being, or a living being. These four conceptions, as we said earlier, relate to different aspects of our attachment. They can be analyzed from different angles through the six perfections. For instance, at the first bhumi, bodhisattvas perfect the perfection of generosity, so we can analyze how to be free from the four conceptions in the context of the perfection of generosity. At the third bhumi, bodhisattvas perfect the perfection of patience, so we can examine how to eradicate the four conceptions from the perspective of the perfection of patience. In brief, when Buddha Shakyamuni was the Sage Forbearance, he had already transcended the four conceptions. If not, he must have had animosity toward the king.

Imagine what we would do if we were in the same situation! We believe we are following the Buddha as the perfect example for us in the path of Dharma study. As *Guide to the Bodhisattva's Way of Life* says, "Just what the Buddha aspired to do in the past, I aspire to do now." We chant this verse every single day, and most often more than once, but have we fulfilled the aspiration? For most people, never mind having their body cut up with a knife, just a careless light bump makes them fly into a rage and even curse. So their daily chanting of generating bodhichitta has become mere lip service to the aspiration.

WHEN ENCOUNTERING UNFAVORABLE CONDITIONS, IT IS BETTER TO PRACTICE PATIENCE

"Therefore, Subhuti, a bodhisattva should be free from any conception while giving rise to the perfect, unsurpassable bodhichitta, and should give rise to bodhichitta neither fixating on form nor fixating on sound, smell, taste, touch, or dharma, but rather should give rise to bodhichitta without fixating on anything. If there is an object to fixate on, it is not a real abiding."

"Fixating" here can be understood as attachment. Ordinary beings have attachment toward everything. However, once they master emptiness, they have no attachment toward real functioning phenomena or unreal phenomena.[9] People who have not yet been exposed to the views of the Middle Way might find this difficult to comprehend. However, those who have already studied the Middle Way would not have a problem. Having integrated conventional bodhichitta and ultimate bodhichitta, the Buddha told us that on the basis of conventional bodhichitta we should also give rise to ultimate bodhichitta, which is the perfect, unsurpassable awakened mind free from any conception. It does not fixate on form, sound, smell, taste, touch, or dharma. As long as there is the least bit of attachment, it is not possible to generate bodhichitta in its real sense.

Relying on this supreme bodhichitta, the Buddha became enlightened. As followers, we should also give rise to such bodhichitta: at the relative level, we benefit countless sentient beings and bear no ill will toward those who harm us; at the ultimate level, since the three spheres are empty by nature, we *give rise to bodhichitta without fixating on anything*. Such bodhichitta would not be deceived by objects but would be in accord with the way things are, which means equal to the state of the Tathagata. As said in the *Shurangama Sutra*, "When objects can be transformed (by your being), it is the same as the Tathagata."

In summary, in order to benefit infinite numbers of sentient beings, the Buddha practiced the perfection of patience within the conventional and has always abided in the wisdom of non-abiding at the ultimate level. We followers should really emulate the Buddha.

In the past, before the four categories of disciples (monks, nuns, male and female laypeople), His Holiness Jigme Phuntsok Rinpoche made this aspiration: "Even if I am harmed by someone through various approaches, I will never harm any sentient being!" This is an ultimate vow of a real practitioner.

To follow the example of our teacher, in the postscript of *The Miserable World* (a book composed by the author to advocate no killing and vegetarian diets), I wrote, "In all my future lives, even if I have to be born as a beggar, I will never become someone who does harm to the life of sentient beings, such as a butcher."

It is of foremost importance for a practitioner to avoid harming sentient beings! Every single day, we make the aspiration aloud, "What the buddhas and bodhisattvas of the past had vowed, I would like to take the same vows." However, if we keep bearing grudges and having animosity toward others, what use is this kind of aspiration?

Of course, ultimately, we should give rise to the ultimate bodhichitta, not fixate on any characteristic, keeping in mind that all phenomena are like dreams and illusions. Chan master Fa Rong of the Tang dynasty said, "The very moment when the mind is placed on something, there is no mind that is placed on anything." When an object is brought into focus, there is actually nothing being focused on. Similarly, at the moment when you are generating bodhichitta, there is nothing being attached to. We should let such wisdom arise.

MASTERING THE PROFOUND EMPTINESS IS PRACTICING BOTH PATIENCE AND GENEROSITY

"Therefore, the Buddha said bodhisattvas should practice generosity without fixating on form."

Here Buddha Shakyamuni quoted a scriptural authority to illuminate this issue—the real generosity of a bodhisattva is free from attachment toward form; it is the perfect generosity with the emptiness of the three spheres.

"Subhuti, in order to benefit all sentient beings, bodhisattvas should practice generosity in such a way."

Whether practicing patience or generosity, bodhisattvas should abide in the state of emptiness of the three spheres. However, within the conventional, in order to benefit sentient beings in the three-thousandfold universe, bodhisattvas should practice material offerings, Dharma offerings, and fearlessness offerings, which include patience or tolerance on profound emptiness.

"The Tathagata said that all characteristics are not characteristics."

The six perfections, no matter whether it is the characteristic of patience or of generosity, can appear like dreams or illusions within the conventional, but under examination with ultimate wisdom, they are not real characteristics.

"Also, sentient beings are not sentient beings."

Without proper analysis, countless sentient beings have been tortured in samsara, the ocean of suffering, but if we scrutinize the matter carefully, sentient beings are not sentient beings, their nature is no different from that of the Buddha.

    Guide to the Bodhisattva's Way of Life also said, "Sentient beings are like dreams and illusions, and when examined they are like plantain trees. Whether they reach nirvana or not, their nature would not change." This means that when examined through ultimate analysis, the essence of all the sentient beings in this world is unborn and unceasing, completely unfindable, just as unreal as the heart of the plantain tree. If this is the case, whether a sentient being enters nirvana or not, their nature would not change a bit.

THE SPEECH OF THE BUDDHA

"Subhuti, what the Tathagata speaks is real, true, as it is, indeceptive, and veritable."

In the ultimate meaning, all phenomena do not exist and are completely insubstantial, but within the conventional they appear like illusions and dreams. Is this statement reasonable? To remove doubt, the Buddha told Subhuti that, unlike ordinary people, the Tathagata's speech is absolutely reliable. This assertion can be sufficiently supported by evidence.

That the Tathagata speaks the reliable truth has been demonstrated in the third chapter of *The Compendium of Valid Cognition*, where it says, "Without that cause, (the Buddha) never lies." The reason the Buddha does not lie is because he has already eliminated any cause for lying—that is, any form of afflictive emotions such as attachment, hatred, and ignorance.

Real
According to the view of Vasubandhu, "real" means that what the Buddha taught within the conventional is real and faultless, such as the karmic law of cause and effect; cyclic existence; the height of Mount Meru; the different universes; the birth, aging, illness, and death of human beings; the intense suffering of cold and heat in the various hells; and so forth. These are beyond the reach of ordinary people's perception, and we can only make assumptions, but the Buddha is able to directly perceive all of these things and teach accordingly.

True
From the perspective of ultimate meaning—in the ultimate reality of basic space, or dharmadhatu—the Tathagata concluded that all phenomena, from form (the first of the five aggregates) up to omniscience, are empty by nature; nothing in dharmadhatu is not empty. This is true speech.

As it is
In the third turning of the wheel of Dharma, the Tathagata inferred that although the essence of all phenomena is empty, buddha nature, or tathagatagarbha, is not absent, is consistently imbued with luminosity and

emptiness, and pervades each sentient being. This truth of the oneness of appearance and emptiness is absolutely reliable, so from the standpoint of suchness, the Buddha speaks as it is, or suchness.

Indeceptive

In order to guide sentient beings, Buddha Shakyamuni gave a great number of Dharma teachings, and each statement has its specific intended meaning. From the time he attained enlightenment until he entered parinirvana, the Buddha never uttered a single deceitful remark. Whereas ordinary people get used to telling lies that harm others as well as themselves, each and every statement the Buddha made is not deceptive and benefits sentient beings both temporarily and ultimately.

Veritable

When the Buddha was turning the wheel of Dharma, a single remark could be taken simultaneously as the language of hungry ghosts, the language of mankind, and so forth when heard by the corresponding kind of sentient beings. Since the Buddha's teachings by their very nature liberate sentient beings, bring the bliss of the higher realms temporarily, and plant the virtuous root for buddhahood ultimately, the speech of the Buddha is the most ultimate.

Sometimes we believe a person is honest and would never tell a lie. However, since the person has not yet eliminated the cause of telling lies, there is still the possibility of giving a false statement for a particular purpose. The Buddha, however, utterly unlike ordinary people, has thoroughly perceived the way things are and eradicated the obscurations of speech, so his speech is perfect.

According to the different capacities of sentient beings, the Buddha sometimes taught the same topic at different levels, but this does not mean the Buddha told lies. We know that textbooks on the same topic for students in universities, middle schools, and elementary schools can present and analyze the same content quite differently; this is because students benefit most by having the information targeted to their cognitive level and capacity. Similarly, in the first, second, and third turnings of the wheel of Dharma, the Buddha certainly taught differently. Clearly, however, his purpose was not to deceive sentient beings but rather to guide them in appropriate stages so that they can reach liberation in the end.

DOES MUTUAL EXISTENCE AND NONEXISTENCE CONTRADICT REASON?

"Subhuti, the Dharma obtained by the Tathagata is neither real nor unreal."

At first glance, this statement sounds incomprehensible because, according to ordinary people's thinking, when "existence" is negated "nonexistence" must take its place, and if "nonexistence" is refuted, "existence" must be correct. The two terms are not mutually exclusive, but only after realizing the nature of all phenomena can we understand how inconceivable this is to the conventional mind.

"The Dharma obtained by the Tathagata" can be explained in different ways. On the one hand, at his causal stage the Tathagata had forsaken his head, eyes, brain, and bone marrow many times, had undergone a great deal of unbearable hardship, and had finally obtained the supreme Dharma of ambrosia. This is the Dharma acquired by the Tathagata.

At the same time, this supreme Dharma of ambrosia is the nature or the ultimate reality of all phenomena, but not anything substantial. When examined by ultimate analysis, the Dharma obtained by the Buddha is unfindable, not real. However, it does not mean nothingness, because in the illusory appearance of sentient beings, the karmic law of cause and effect, and the suffering of cyclic existence, the difficulty of obtaining human existence and so forth do exist.

All phenomena are neither existent nor nonexistent. This fact has profound connotations. Within the conventional, dreamlike and illusory appearance is real, not nonexistent; before the duality of subject and object dissolves into dharmadhatu, all these phenomena exist. However, at the ultimate level, there are no substantial things at all.

As said in *The Four Hundred Stanzas on the Middle Way*, "Anything that exists within the conventional does not exist at the ultimate level." Therefore, from the conventional perspective, all phenomena are not unreal, though when analyzed with transcendental wisdom, all phenomena are not real.

"Subhuti, if a bodhisattva practices generosity while fixating on form, it is just as a person in a dark room cannot see anything. If a bodhisattva practices generosity without fixating on form, it is just as a person with healthy eyes under the sunshine can see various forms."

When bodhisattvas practice generosity while abiding in the state of the emptiness of the three spheres, it is the most perfect generosity. Regardless of which perfection is practiced, it must be imbued with the perfection of wisdom. Otherwise, the practice would be like a blind person groping in darkness—the ultimate reality cannot be found. *The Great Treatise on the Perfection of Wisdom* says, "The five perfections are like a blind man, the perfection of transcendental wisdom is like eyes that see clearly."

The Introduction to the Middle Way states:

> A single man endowed with eyes
> can lead unseeing multitudes with ease to where they wish to go.
> And so it is with wisdom, here;
> it takes the sightless virtues, guiding them to victory.
>   (chapter 6, verse 2)

Master Yong Jia also said, "When one fixates on characteristics while practicing generosity, it only accumulates merit to be born in the god realm; afterward, unfavorable things await. This is like shooting an arrow into the sky: when the force exhausts, the arrow will fall."

The *Diamond Cutter Sutra* examines mainly the merit of transcendental wisdom. Ultimately speaking, the first five perfections are analogous to a blind man walking around. In the end, it is through the perfection of transcendental wisdom that one can finally reach the other shore of liberation.

How About Reciting the *Diamond Cutter Sutra* Once a Day for the Rest of Your Life?

"Subhuti, in a future time, if a son or daughter of noble qualities is able to uphold and recite this sutra, with his Buddha's wisdom, the Tathagata can completely understand and perceive that this person will certainly attain countless and boundless merit."

According to the view of *Abhidharmakosha*, unlike the listener and the self-realizer, the Buddha is able to clearly perceive the entire three-thousandfold universe in one instant; moreover, with his clairvoyance he can also vividly see the development of everything in the future hundreds of thousands of eons. Therefore, right now, we are studying the *Diamond Cutter Sutra*, and in the future we are going to obtain inconceivable merit. The Buddha already clearly perceived this long ago.

Having limited intelligence, some people find they are unable to study, contemplate, or meditate on the *Diamond Cutter Sutra*; however, they still persevere in reciting it once every day, which creates enormous merit. Mipham Rinpoche once said, "If one does not have the ability to listen, reflect, and meditate, it is better to chant genuine vajra words." Moreover, chanting sutras is one of the ten Dharma conducts (*dasa dharma caryah*)—that is, transcribing, offering, giving, listening, reading, upholding, teaching, chanting, contemplating, and meditating. Any one of the ten conducts can create immeasurable merit.

Even just transcribing or listening to one verse could generate merit that surpasses any worldly virtuous root. If we could aspire to chant the *Diamond Cutter Sutra* once every day for the rest of our life, this human existence we have obtained will fulfill its meaning.

Obviously, once we make the promise, we should keep it. No matter what happens, we should not give up our resolve. In *The Biographies of Great Masters*, Master Wei Gong of the Tang dynasty never interrupted his chanting of the *Diamond Cutter Sutra*, fifty times every day for over thirty years. At the time of death, he was reborn in the Pure Land of Great Bliss without any obstacles.

It might be a bit hard for us to chant the *Diamond Cutter Sutra* fifty times a day; however, to chant it once every day should not be a problem.

15. The Merit of Upholding This Sutra

FAITH IN THE *DIAMOND CUTTER SUTRA* CREATES GREATER MERIT THAN BODY OFFERING

NEXT, through analogy, the Buddha illustrated that it is of immeasurable merit to uphold and chant the *Diamond Cutter Sutra*.

"Subhuti, if a son or daughter of noble qualities gave away his or her body as many times as the number of sand grains in the Ganges River in the morning, midday, and afternoon, respectively, for as long as hundreds and thousands of billions and trillions of eons, and if someone else gained irreversible faith after hearing the Diamond Cutter Sutra, *the merit of the latter would far surpass that of the former. There is no need to mention that if someone transcribes, upholds, chants, or elaborates it to others, the merit would be even more immeasurable."*

In comparison to material offerings, body offerings create hundreds of thousands of times more merit. As said in *The Words of My Perfect Teacher*, only bodhisattvas at the first or above bhumis are capable of giving away bodies; ordinary people cannot do this directly, so it has supreme merit. Putting aside giving away one's body countless times, just a couple of times can accumulate inconceivable merit. However, when compared with Dharma offerings, countless body offerings cannot surpass in merit one instant of faith in the teachings of emptiness.

If gaining irreversible faith when hearing this sutra can accumulate such supreme merit, there is no need to mention the merit gained in transcribing, upholding, reciting, or elaborating it to others. These series of acts are called "Dharma offerings." The *Sutra on Upasaka Precepts* says, "If one provides paper and ink and asks others to transcribe, or if one transcribes oneself, the authentic scriptures of the Tathagata, and then gives them away to other people and asks them to recite the scripture, this is called

'Dharma offering.'" In ancient times, it was common to transcribe sutras by hand; nowadays with the printing industry so developed, handwriting is no longer required, so printing scriptures or distributing Dharma books for free is also a genuine Dharma offering.

Among all forms of generosity, Dharma offerings are the most supreme; therefore, transcribing, reciting, and elaborating the *Diamond Cutter Sutra* creates inconceivable merit. If we could practice accordingly, we could iron out any tribulation that befalls us. Take this hunter's story, for example. Once there was a hunter who had recited only one chapter of the *Diamond Cutter Sutra*. After falling into hells, he was exempt from intensive torture and experienced only some minor suffering.

ONLY PEOPLE WHO HAVE GENERATED MAHAYANA BODHICHITTA ARE THE TARGETED AUDIENCE OF THIS SUTRA

"Subhuti, in concise words, this sutra is of inconceivable, immeasurable, and infinite merit."

To summarize the above, the Buddha told Subhuti that the merit of the *Diamond Cutter Sutra* cannot be pondered with conceptual thought nor expressed in the language of ordinary people; it cannot be comprehended even by the wisdom of arhats.

"The Tathagata taught this for the followers of the Great Vehicle, the Supreme Vehicle. If someone could uphold, chant, or elaborate the Diamond Cutter Sutra *to others, the Tathagata would completely know and perceive that this person would attain immeasurable, indescribable, infinite, and inconceivable merit. Such people would achieve the perfect unsurpassable enlightenment of the Tathagata."*

Since the *Diamond Cutter Sutra* is mainly about emptiness, the origin of all the buddhas and bodhisattvas, ordinary beings are unable to digest it. Therefore, before giving teachings, the Tathagata would first examine if the audience members were suitable Dharma vessels; it turns out only those who have generated bodhichitta are qualified to receive this teaching. Take Subhuti as an example. As mentioned in many sutras, he appeared as an arhat of the Basic Vehicle but in fact had the capacity of the Great

Vehicle. So it is clear that the Tathagata intended to teach the *Diamond Cutter Sutra* for Great Vehicle followers.

Next, why is the merit so immense for those upholding, reciting, and elaborating the *Diamond Cutter Sutra* to others? The reason is that the blessing power of the Buddha is inconceivable and the supremeness of the Dharma is inconceivable. As said in the *Sadhana of the Sutra on Recollecting the Three Jewels*, "The merit of the Tathagata is inconceivable, the merit of the Dharma is inconceivable, and the merit of the Sangha is inconceivable; once faith has been gained in the inconceivable merit fields, one gains inconceivable rewards."

It is written that when Vasubandhu chanted the *Sutra of the Transcendental Wisdom*, a pigeon nesting on the roof often listened to him. Through the merit of hearing this sutra, after its death the pigeon was reborn as a man. Later he took ordination and became a great master, known as Sthiramati (c. 510–70).

Moreover, according to the *Records of Mount Wutai*, there was a monk called Hui Qian in the Tang dynasty. In order to find a mountain spring, he chanted the *Diamond Cutter Sutra* for ten thousand days unceasingly. In the end, a spring really emerged, and it is said that whoever drinks from it or bathes in it will realize wisdom. When His Holiness Jigme Phuntsok Rinpoche visited this "Spring of Prajna" at Mount Wutai, he also drank the water.

WHO CANNOT TAKE IN THE *DIAMOND CUTTER SUTRA*?

People who uphold and recite the *Diamond Cutter Sutra* are bound to obtain boundless merit and reach the unsurpassable buddhahood. What is the reason?

"Why? Subhuti, those who are interested in lesser principles grasp the conception of a self, a person, a sentient being, and a living being, so they would not hear, comprehend, recite, or elucidate this sutra to others."

Interested in lesser principles
In comparison to the Great Vehicle, "lesser principles" refers to worldly principles, teachings of the Basic Vehicle, or teachings that aim at self-liberation. Those who are interested in lesser principles grasp the

conception of a self, a person, a sentient being, and a living being; therefore, when it comes to the *Diamond Cutter Sutra*, they cannot first listen to
it, then recite it, or finally explain it to others.

We should understand that people who cling to characteristics are not
Dharma vessels for prajna or transcendental wisdom. As it said in the *Sutra
of Transcendental Wisdom*, "Whoever clings to the true existence of phenomena cannot reach the liberation of the three levels of enlightenment."
Why is that? Because these people have few virtuous roots and associate
with lots of wicked companions, so they cannot gain faith in the vast and
profound teachings.

As said in the *Ornament of the Great Vehicle Sutras*, "Due to their inferior
faith and elements, they would not comprehend the vast and profound
Dharma." Therefore the Buddha didn't teach the *Diamond Cutter Sutra*
before those "interested in lesser principles," for even if he did, they would
not be able to digest it.

Since people interested in lesser principles are not suitable Dharma
vessels to study the *Diamond Cutter Sutra*, some great masters believe this
indirectly suggests that in order to receive prajna teachings, the audience
has to meet higher criterion. To teach it to immature audiences may cause
them to slander it because they are not mentally ready to receive it. Therefore, when spreading the Buddhadharma, we should examine the capacity
of the audience and then give teachings accordingly.

THE *DIAMOND CUTTER SUTRA* IS ALSO A STUPA

*"Subhuti, wherever this sutra is present, all the worldly gods, humans, and asuras
should make offerings. Understand that this place has become a stupa, worthy
of respecting, paying homage to, circumambulating, and filling with flowers and
fragrance."*

After the Buddha entered parinirvana, stupas were erected to represent
the mind of the Buddha. In Buddhism, there are eight kinds of buddha
stupas, and wherever a stupa exists, followers should pay homage. As said
in *Guide to the Bodhisattva's Way of Life*, "Paying homage to the stupa of
the Buddha is the root of bodhichitta." As great masters in the past have
said, for people who uphold, chant, and practice the *Sutra of Prajna*, even

the dirt and dust they step on have always been paid homage to by Indra and Brahma.

We have an interesting account regarding "understand that this place has become a stupa." Under the reign of Hong Zhi in the Tang dynasty, the Suchness Stupa at Cheng Tian Temple was about to collapse, but a monk named Hui Lin spent twenty years raising funds and having it restored. What was the cause of his intention to rebuild the stupa?

Once when Hui Lin was meditating, two messengers of the Lord of Death suddenly showed up, put a lasso around his neck, and attempted to drag him to see the Lord of Death. Hui Lin beseeched them for a grace period of seven days in order to finish Buddhist ceremonies for liberating blazing-mouth hungry ghosts, and the messengers agreed.

Upon their departure, he gathered his disciples and asked, "The Lord of Death wants me in seven days, what suggestions do you have?"

A disciple said, "About one day's ship ride from here there is a Cheng Tian Temple in Suzhou. A Chan master there practices on the *Diamond Cutter Sutra* exclusively. He has incomparable might, you should turn to him for help."

Immediately, Hui Lin left to find the Chan master and told him what happened as soon as he arrived. The Chan master answered, "If you promise me to restore this collapsing stupa, I have a method to save your life." Without hesitation, Hui Lin committed to do it.

Afterward, the Chan master told him to recite the *Diamond Cutter Sutra* without interruption for seven whole days, and at the end of every recitation to say, "Understand that this place has become a stupa."

Following this instruction, Hui Lin chanted the sutra diligently day and night, without a break or sleep.

Seven days later, the two messengers showed up again. When they asked the whereabouts of Hui Lin, the Chan master said, "In my room." They entered the room and saw only a giant stupa radiating brilliant light rays, but no Hui Lin.

Unable to accomplish their task, they went to ask the Chan master, "Hui Lin agreed to go with us today, but we cannot find him, what should we do?" The Chan master replied, "It is the might of prajna that prevents you from approaching him, you'd better give it up." Hearing this, the two messengers left in a huff.

Then the Chan master said to Hui Lin, "I have saved your life, you should keep your promise to raise funds and restore the stupa." Hui Lin kept his promise and raised funds every day, and finally, after twenty years, an extremely sublime stupa was erected.

As we can see, the *Diamond Cutter Sutra* is indeed mighty. People who really have no time to chant it should consider carrying one around with them. I myself have gained enormous faith in the *Diamond Cutter Sutra* and now plan to always carry with me a tiny *Diamond Cutter Sutra* with my *Liberation through Wearing*.

When you have the *Diamond Cutter Sutra*, on the one hand, demons and non-humans are unable to harm you; on the other hand, when other people pay respect or homage to you, it won't deplete your merit because you have a stupa with you.

16. It Can Purify Karmic Obscurations

EVERY UNFAVORABLE CONDITION IS ACTUALLY A FAVORABLE CONDITION

"Again, Subhuti, if a son or daughter of noble qualities who upholds and recites the Diamond Cutter Sutra *encounters disdain, it is because they are supposed to fall into lower realms on account of their previous misdeeds. However, just by experiencing disrespect from others, they are able to purify their previous misdeeds and attain perfect, unsurpassable enlightenment."*

Upholds and recites

IN THE Tibetan edition and Xuan Zang's translation it says, "uphold, recite, thoroughly master, and explain to others and contemplate accordingly."

Kumarajiva's translation is the same as Yi Jing's. In Xuan Zang's translation, it also says, "If encountering disdain, or extreme insult, what is the reason? Subhuti, it is because these sentient beings have created impure karma in their past lives, and because of that they are supposed to fall into the lower realms. However, through experiencing disdain in their present life, all impure karma of past lives will be exhausted and they will attain the perfect, unsurpassable enlightenment."

People who regularly recite the *Diamond Cutter Sutra* often find they encounter more unfavorable conditions, are insulted by others, are unable to get along with some people, face obstacles in their path of practice, and so forth. These circumstances seem unfavorable, but indeed they are favorable conditions because they can purify karmic obscuration and speed up the process of reaching enlightenment.

People often complain, "I have been a Buddhist for years, but why are there more and more unfavorable conditions in my life? Does the Buddha have no power of blessing?" Their doubts are unreasonable. The *Diamond Cutter Sutra* tells you here: you are supposed to fall into the lower realms to suffer intensively, but through the merit of upholding this sutra, all your karmic obscurations are eradicated. The *Sutra on Liberation* also says, "Even the misdeed that could drag you down into the lower realms can be purified just by experiencing a headache."

Some Buddhist beginners believe unfavorable conditions are inauspicious, so they refuse to accept them, not knowing that unfavorable conditions can purify karmic obscurations.

When reading the *Lotus Sutra*, Emperor Ren Zong of the Song dynasty said:

> Nectar trickles through my throat,
> butter drips in my mouth,
> when only a couple of lines in the *Lotus Sutra* are explained,
> even the misdeeds as grave as mountains can be completely purified.

This is also true for the *Diamond Cutter Sutra*. By reciting the *Diamond Cutter Sutra*, even misdeeds as monstrous as mountains can be completely purified because it is the essential wisdom of all the buddhas and bodhisattvas. If one realizes the nature of karmic obscuration through this sutra, any kind of misdeed is able to be purified without a trace.

Master Yong Jia also said, "Once one realizes (its nature), karmic obscuration is empty by nature, without realizing (its nature), one has to pay back previous karmic debt." Therefore when unfavorable conditions appear, we should not always think this is bad, but rather realize it is a way to dispel sufferings awaiting in future lives; without experiencing these minor hardships, we have to suffer much more in future lives.

Every time he hears that a great master is ill or has some unfavorable condition in their enlightened activities, Khenpo Legshe (Legs bshad), from Domang Monastery, always uses this scriptural authority, "When unfavorable conditions befall great masters, it is a sign of their future liberation."

Therefore whoever has generated bodhichitta should not be too concerned when unfavorable conditions befall. Isn't it a great deal to substitute the intense pains of the lower realms in future lives for some slight bitterness in this present life?

NEVER BE SEPARATED FROM THE BUDDHA
IN ALL LIFETIMES

"Subhuti, I can recall countless eons ago before I met Buddha Dipankara, I had met eighty-four billion and trillions of tathagatas, I made offerings to them, served them as attendants, and never took their words in vain."

As for the merit of making offerings to the Buddha, the *Lotus Sutra* says, "If someone makes an offering of one flower before an image of the Buddha, even absent-mindedly, he or she will gradually see countless buddhas." If this is the case, the merit would be inconceivably greater if one makes offerings to and attends countless buddhas. However, no matter how immense this merit is, when compared with reciting the *Diamond Cutter Sutra*, it is rather inferior.

"Again, if someone upholds and recites this sutra in the time of degeneration, when compared to his merit, my merit of offering countless buddhas is less than one hundredth, one billionth, or one trillionth of his, and cannot even be measured or described with similes."

Buddhist scriptures are incomprehensible and even inconceivable to conceptual thought. I often think, "Our conceptual thoughts cannot fathom the karmic law of cause and effect within the conventional, let alone the profound meaning of sutras. The wisdom and merit of the Buddha is indeed unimaginable!"

Here the sutras reemphasize the merit of Dharma offerings and also explain the inconceivable merit of the *Diamond Cutter Sutra*. Why is the merit so immense? As the *Jewel Heap Sutra* says, "Mantras, sublime medicines, secret prescriptions, and the power of dependent origination are inconceivable; similarly, the merit of skillful means, meditative concentration, clairvoyance, and the conduct of buddhas and bodhisattvas is also inconceivable." Since the wisdom of the Buddha is inconceivable and this sutra was taught based on the Buddha's wisdom, the merit must be inconceivable.

What on earth is merit or virtue? The *Sixth Patriarch Platform Sutra* says, "Not being separated from nature is merit, not contaminated in application is virtue. Seeing the nature is merit, abiding in equality is virtue."

Through upholding and reciting the *Diamond Cutter Sutra*, one could attain the state of equality and immaculacy; this is genuine merit and virtue, which far surpasses contaminated virtue at the conventional level.

Master Han Shan also said, "Whoever realizes prajna (transcendental wisdom) can suddenly be reborn in the Buddha family in as short a time as one thought, and will never be separated from the Buddha in all lifetimes, so this merit is most supreme."

"PROFOUND DHARMA UNFATHOMABLE TO ME IS NOT NECESSARILY INCOMPREHENSIBLE TO THE BUDDHA"

"Subhuti, if a son or daughter of noble qualities upholds and recites this sutra in the future, if I elaborate on their merit, upon hearing it, some people might go insane, or doubt it and have misgivings."

As we can see, the Buddha had prophesied that in the degeneration time there would be people who slander the teachings of the Great Vehicle. Some learned people have firm faith in the Buddha's words, often cite the Buddha's words, and always praise the merit of the Buddha. As the sutra says, "Therefore, the wise strongly believe in the words of the Buddha, use the Buddha's wisdom as authority, and praise the knowledge of the Buddha in their speech." However, those lacking wisdom suspect the supreme merit of the *Diamond Cutter Sutra* and even slander it recklessly.

The Ornament of the Great Vehicle Sutras says, "Profound Dharma unfathomable to me is not necessarily incomprehensible to the Buddha." This remark has profound connotation, so please savor it repeatedly and cultivate firm faith without any doubt in the words of the Buddha.

When you cannot comprehend something in the Buddhist scriptures, do not unscrupulously comment on it with conceptual thoughts (such as "this is wrong, that is right"), but rather pray often to the lama and the Three Jewels. If you can follow my advice, wisdom will gradually arise in your being and you will realize the ultimate meaning of the Buddha.

BEARING GREAT EFFECTS FROM SMALL CAUSES

"Subhuti, understand that the meaning of this sutra is inconceivable, the effect ripening from it is also inconceivable."

Through the blessing of Buddhist sutras, our suffering and afflictive emotions can be suddenly eradicated. This is indeed inconceivable. Moreover, each part of a Buddhist sutra has its outer, inner, and secret connotations, respectively. This uniqueness is also inconceivable. In addition, if one sincerely prays to Buddhist sutras, one absolutely attains blessings from the Buddha, so the effect is also inconceivable.

We can also find sutras that point out other inconceivables. The *Sutra Requested by Naga King Anavatapta* says, "Sentient beings are inconceivable, so the merit of generating bodhichitta based on them is also inconceivable."

The *Lamp Offering Sutra* says, "The merit of gaining faith in sutras is inconceivable, bearing great effects through small causes is inconceivable, the capacity of sentient beings is inconceivable, the might of the Three Jewels is inconceivable."

Since the *Diamond Cutter Sutra* has such supreme merit, when chanting it we'd better apply the six methods, such as mind chanting, vajra chanting, silent chanting, and so forth. Merely glancing along the words while uttering them does not necessarily create such immense merit. Therefore while chanting the sutra, we should ponder its meaning. Even if we ponder for just one moment, the merit of doing so is boundless because the meaning of the sutra is inconceivable.

We should be aware that our life is transient. In this limited time frame, we should give up meaningless trivia. Even if we should live for only one day, cherish that time to read sutras and commentaries because their meaning is inconceivable. As a result, the merit and the ripened effect through this action will also be inconceivable.

17. Ultimate Selflessness

THE *DIAMOND CUTTER SUTRA* IS ALL ABOUT TAMING ONE'S MIND

FROM HERE ON, the content is mainly on the merit of this sutra. This is relatively easy to understand, and the explanation is consistent with what has been covered earlier. Therefore in the past when great masters taught this sutra, they expounded the previous chapters in great detail but from here on their commentary was quite brief.

Then Subhuti said to the Buddha, "Bhagavan, after a son or daughter of noble qualities generates the perfect, unsurpassable bodhichitta, how do they abide? How do they tame their mind?"

Mind is the root of all phenomena. The Buddha gave 84,000 teachings and the key for each teaching is to tame one's mind. Of course, there are different levels of achievement: compared with worldly people, religious followers are more easily able to tame their minds; compared with religious followers, arhats have more pliant minds; compared with arhats, bodhisattvas have more peaceful minds; and compared with bodhisattvas, buddhas have the most perfect minds.

In brief, Subhuti again asked the following questions before the Buddha: Since the ultimate goal of generating bodhichitta is to tame one's mind, initially, how should one settle one's mind? In the middle, how should one practice? And finally, what kind of result will one reach?

These series of questions are crucial to the *Diamond Cutter Sutra*, which is mainly about how to tame one's mind and how to accumulate merit within the conventional. We recite and uphold the *Diamond Cutter Sutra* every day, which only helps to tame one's mind at the conventional level. At the ultimate level, only when our minds reach perfect peace or nirvana can it be called the "ultimate tame mind."

CONVENTIONAL AND ULTIMATE BODHICHITTA

The Buddha told Subhuti, "When a son or daughter of noble qualities generates the perfect, unsurpassable bodhichitta, they should give rise to the thought: 'I should liberate all sentient beings, and although all sentient beings are liberated, there is no single sentient being that has really been liberated.'"

To answer Subhuti's questions, the Buddha replied that there are so many approaches to taming the mind, but the ultimate and supreme method is to generate bodhichitta.

Patrul Rinpoche once said, "With it [bodhichitta], everything is complete; without it, everything is missing." When we have bodhichitta, we have accomplished everything, there is no need to engage in any other practice. However, if we do not have bodhichitta, any other practice cannot succeed.

Here, the Buddha told Subhuti, in order to tame one's mind, we must generate the conventional and ultimate bodhichitta. What is conventional bodhichitta? Recall the directive given in the third chapter: "I should liberate all sentient beings." This is because all sentient beings in cyclic existence have been my parents before, but now they have sunk in the suffering ocean of samsara, I must exert myself to liberate them and place them in buddhahood. Such motivation is conventional bodhichitta, which in turn breaks into aspiration bodhichitta and action bodhichitta. These are the best methods to tame one's mind at the relative level.

At the absolute level, "Although all sentient beings are liberated, there is no single sentient being that has really been liberated." Both the objects that need to be liberated and the subject that is able to liberate sentient beings have no intrinsic existence. This is the ultimate bodhichitta.

As practitioners, when examining any phenomenon we must distinguish the two truths, conventional truth and ultimate truth. Chandrakirti once said, "Since phenomena can be seen as reality and delusion, there are ultimate truth and conventional truth." Based on this, bodhichitta also falls into two types: ultimate and conventional.

In order to master relative truth and ultimate truth, the correct order is also required: first the relative truth, then the ultimate truth. That is to say, we should first generate conventional bodhichitta; when it is perfected, we should keep in mind it is not the final stage and then generate ultimate bodhichitta imbued with prajnaparamita. Through this skillful means, one is bound to have a tame mind.

ALL CHARACTERISTICS ARE ILLUSORY

"Subhuti, if bodhisattvas have the conception of a self, a person, a sentient being, and a living being, they are not real bodhisattvas."

All characteristics are illusory, they do not inherently exist. *The Fundamental Wisdom of the Middle Way* also says:

> As said in the sutra,
> (all phenomena) are illusive delusions and mistakenly grasped
>   characteristics;
> since all conditioned phenomena are wrongly grasped,
> they are all illusive delusions.
> If bodhisattvas attach to the four characteristics,
> their motivation is not ultimate, and they are not real bodhisattvas.
> (chapter 13, verse 1)

"Why? Subhuti, there is no dharma that generates the perfect, unsurpassable bodhichitta."

The Buddha has been versed in the ultimate reality of all phenomena. Before his wisdom, not even the smallest phenomenon is observable. If there are phenomena findable in ultimate reality, buddhas and bodhisattvas are supposed to observe them. However, since nothing is findable when examined with their ultimate wisdom, those who have generated bodhichitta to reach the perfect, unsurpassable enlightenment do not exist. Therefore, bodhichitta itself also lacks inherent existence. So this is called ultimate bodhichitta.

The *Lankavatara Sutra* also says, "Since existence and nonexistence do not arise, all phenomena do not arise." At the ultimate level, neither existence nor nonexistence exists, so all phenomena have the great emptiness of non-arising.

EVEN THE BUDDHA HAS NEVER RECEIVED
ANY DHARMA

Next, Buddha Shakyamuni explained this principle using his personal experience.

"Subhuti, what do you think? Before Buddha Dipankara, had the Tathagata obtained the Dharma called the 'perfect, unsurpassable enlightenment'?"

"No, Bhagavan. From my understanding of what the Buddha taught, the Buddha never obtained the Dharma called the 'perfect, unsurpassable enlightenment' before Buddha Dipankara."

The Buddha said, "Thus it is. Thus it is. Subhuti, there is indeed no such Dharma that led the Tathagata to attain the perfect, unsurpassable enlightenment."

Thus it is, thus it is

There are two ways to explain these words. First, the Buddha was very satisfied with Subhuti's answer, so he praised him by agreeing twice. Second, Subhuti said the Buddha had never obtained the Dharma in ultimate reality, which indirectly suggests that the Buddha had acquired the Dharma within the conventional: the Buddha uttered "thus it is" twice, once to agree on his understanding at the ultimate level and once to confirm that this is like an illusion within the conventional.

Subhuti's answer is accurate. In the nature of ultimate reality, nothing is findable and the Tathagata had never attained the perfect, unsurpassable enlightenment.

The *Sutra of the Virtuous Eon* records that at his causal stage, Buddha Shakyamuni made offerings of sublime clothes before Buddha Mahashakya, and this aspiration: "Sugata, as you possess your body, retinue, longevity, pure land, and supreme major and minor marks, may we too attain the state equal to yours." This is a description at the conventional level. Nagarjuna also said, "The nature of the Tathagata is the nature of the world." But at the ultimate level, the Tathagata has never obtained any Dharma.

ALL PHENOMENA ARISE FROM CAUSES AND CONDITIONS

"Subhuti, if there was the Dharma that the Tathagata had obtained to reach the perfect, unsurpassable enlightenment, the Buddha Dipankara would never have prophesied: 'In a future life, you will become a buddha named Shakyamuni.'"

Ninety-one eons ago, the Bhagavan was born as a brahmin named Virtuous Wisdom (another account says a great monk named Dharma Cloud). In that lifetime, he attained a tolerance toward the non-arising of all phenomena before Buddha Dipankara, who bestowed him this prophecy: "In the future, you will become a buddha named Shakyamuni who will liberate countless sentient beings in Sahalokadhatu."

This account did happen within the conventional, but if we grasp that this also exists at the ultimate level, and the Dharma that the Buddha had obtained exists, then Buddha Dipankara would have never made such prophecy. Why is that? If there were one truly existing Dharma, its nature should be changeless, everlasting. It would be impossible to appear like illusions or dreams in the future, nor could it manifest in the present. It is the prophecy of Buddha Dipankara that all phenomena dependently originate from causes and conditions, lacking inherent existence, as has been shown.

THIS WAS HOW BUDDHA SHAKYAMUNI CAME INTO BEING

"Because of the nonexistence of the perfect, unsurpassable enlightenment, Buddha Dipankara prophesied, 'In a future life, you will become a buddha named Shakyamuni.'"

Only when one has truly realized that nothing is findable at the ultimate level can one obtain illusion-like prophecy within the conventional.

As recorded in the *One Hundred Karmic Stories*, in his causal stage, at the first sight of Buddha Dipankara, Buddha Shakyamuni was in ecstasy. Seeing that the road was muddy, he spread his hair on the ground and said, "If I will be able to reach enlightenment and widely turn the wheel of Dharma, Lord Buddha, please walk through on my hair."

As expected, Buddha Dipankara stepped on his hair and prophesied: "In the future, you will obtain liberation and realize the perfect, unsurpassable enlightenment as Buddha Shakyamuni, and you will become the only lamp of the cyclic existence of the three realms."

If the prophecy given by the Buddha existed in the ultimate reality, it would not be a real prophecy. In his *Commentary on the Ornament of the Middle Way*, Mipham Rinpoche said that among all the objects to be known, if there were one truly existent object, all objects would never appear; it is because none of them truly exists that it is tenable to have various objects appear. Think of the reflections of mountains and rivers in a mirror: it is because they are not truly existent that they are able to be reflected in a small mirror. Likewise, it is because all phenomena lack inherent existence that they are able to appear. This is the nature of all phenomena.

While reading this sutra you might feel that sometimes it admits existence and sometimes it refutes existence; sometimes it says that prophecy was obtained and sometimes it says that prophecy had never been received. It sounds contradictory and inconsistent. However, if you calm your mind and ponder it, you will find the inconceivable state it introduces and your mind will have an unprecedented experience.

Nowadays many commentaries on the *Diamond Cutter Sutra* are available. I have read and listened to many of them. Some are polished in expression, and some sound very soothing, but when the actual meaning is examined and one finds that in some places the meaning has not been clearly elucidated, it might be because the teaching transmission has not been passed on to the commentators. Nevertheless, I believe these various explanations are skillful means used by buddhas and bodhisattvas in different forms to liberate sentient beings. Ultimately, there must be no difference between the commentaries.

Here I have tried to clarify the intended meaning of the sutra. I don't claim I have explained it thoroughly, but rather I am just trying to inspire more valuable elaborations.

WHAT IS THE MEANING OF "TATHAGATA"?

Earlier, we found that if Buddha Shakyamuni truly exists, he would not have received the prophecy of his future buddhahood; only when he does not truly exist can his future buddhahood be prophesied. This statement appears unfathomable, but why is that?

"Why? The Tathagata is how things really are."

"Tathagata" is one of the ten titles of the Buddha. It means "one who has thus gone." "Thus" means suchness, which refers to the ultimate nature of dharmadhatu, or the basic space; "gone" means having reached such a state. According to the interpretation in Tibetan Buddhism, Tathagata means having thoroughly reached the state of suchness.

The so-called suchness, or "reality as it is," as defined in *The Discourse on the Perfection of Consciousness Only* is: "'Reality' means real, not delusive; 'as it is' means everlasting, without change." Shravakas, bodhisattvas, and buddhas have realized different levels of suchness; only buddhas have thoroughly realized the ultimate nature of reality as it is.

Here, the titles Tathagata and True Suchness are interchangeable because the Tathagata is not a figure with eyes and nose but the nature of all phenomena. This ultimate reality is genuine Tathagata and is unable to receive prophecy.

How things really are

The true face of all phenomena is thus. From the perspective of emptiness, no matter if buddhas and bodhisattvas come to the human realm or not, the nature of phenomena would never change. This is also the reason why the *Diamond Cutter Sutra* is so profound.

"If someone says, 'The Tathagata has attained the perfect, unsurpassable enlightenment,' Subhuti, the fact is there is no Dharma that leads the Buddha to attain the perfect, unsurpassable enlightenment."

Here the translations by Xuan Zang and Yi Jing differ slightly from Kumarajiva's. Xuan Zang translates the passage thus: "If it is said that 'the one who thus comes, worthy of offering, the one who has attained complete enlightenment, can realize the perfect, unsurpassable enlightenment,' then this statement is untrue." Yi Jing: "If it is said that the Tathagata attained the perfect, unsurpassable enlightenment, it is false speech."

The Tibetan edition says, "Subhuti, if someone says that the Tathagata attained the perfect, unsurpassable enlightenment, this person has already entered a wrong path." If you decide to study the *Diamond Cutter Sutra*, I recommend you compare the existing translations: the comparison helps you understand the sutra better. When a passage is vague in one translation, you will very likely find a clearer description in another edition.

For ordinary people who have not yet realized ultimate reality, it is tenable to admit that the Tathagata attained complete enlightenment before their deluded sensory faculty and consciousness. Even the Buddha himself said that he attained enlightenment at Bodh Gaya: "I have attained the ambrosia of unconditioned Dharma, and it is profound, peaceful, and free from stains; since no sentient beings are able to understand it, I will just stay quietly at a peaceful place."

Therefore, at the conventional level, the Buddha manifested before sentient beings as follows: at the beginning, generated bodhichitta; in the middle, practiced the six perfections and ten thousand actions; and in the end, realized the union of dharmakaya, or truth body, and rupakaya, or form body, and indeed attained the perfect, unsurpassable enlightenment. However, at the ultimate level these are all unreal and unfindable.

REAL IN A DREAM, UNREAL WHEN AWAKE

"Subhuti, the perfect, unsurpassable enlightenment attained by the Tathagata is neither real nor unreal."

In the conventional sense, Buddha Shakyamuni had subjugated demons, attained enlightenment at Bodh Gaya, and turned the wheel of Dharma at Deer Park and other places in India. These are all incontrovertible facts. However, at the ultimate level, all appearances do not exist. The *King of Meditative Concentration Sutra* says, "Just as a man dreamed of an exceedingly beautiful woman and had strong lust for her, but when he awoke nothing was actually there, we should understand that all phenomena share the same attribute (neither real at the ultimate level nor unreal at the conventional level)."

The nature of all phenomena is neither real nor unreal. But most people have not mastered this principle, nor have they heard the teachings on emptiness, so they often fall to extremes. Some people believe nothing exists—the karmic law of cause and effect does not exist, generating bodhichitta does not exist—while others believe that everything truly exists—the Tathagata is a sacred saint with all the virtues, he truly exists. People with these views have entered the wrong path, unable to see the true face of the Tathagata.

Earlier in the sutra it says that the meaning of the sutra is inconceivable and the result from the sutra is also inconceivable. Here it says the perfect, unsurpassable enlightenment is neither real nor unreal. These vajra words can lead to inconceivably great results, so we all should remember this line! In fact, we should say that "neither real nor unreal" contains the truth of the entire universe and life. Whatever we examine, it is not unreal within the conventional—for instance, if we think that after committing misdeeds, suffering is bound to befall; likewise, it is not real at the ultimate level. This is the truth of all phenomena.

ARE MURDER AND ARSON BUDDHADHARMA?

"Thus the Tathagata said all phenomena are Buddhadharma."

In the *Manjushri Sutra*, the Bodhisattva Manjushri asked Shariputra, "What is the most supreme Buddhadharma?" Shariputra answered, "All phenomena are of no essence is the most supreme Buddhadharma." As we can see, no dharma is not Buddhadharma. The Buddhadharma pervades all phenomena.

In China, an emperor's teacher named Hui Zhong once said while giving a teaching on the *Diamond Cutter Sutra*, "All phenomena are Buddhadharma." A disciple asked, "If everything is Buddhadharma, are murder and arson Buddhadharma?" Laughing, the master replied, "Murder and arson are also empty by nature, so they are Buddhadharma."

At the conventional level, Buddhadharma draws a clear line between what to adopt and what to abandon—murder and arson are misdeeds that should be abandoned. However, at the ultimate level nothing needs to be adopted or abandoned. Thus we have the answer to the question from the perspectives of the two truths, respectively. Master Hui Zhong didn't distinguish between them; he answered the question mainly from the view of the ultimate meaning.

"Subhuti, all phenomena, so called, is not all phenomena, so it is all phenomena."

In order to eradicate the desire, hatred, and ignorance of sentient beings and lead them onto the path of enlightenment, the Buddha turned the wheel of Dharma three times and gave eighty-four thousand Dharma teachings at different times. However, in the nature of ultimate reality, these teachings are not in the nature of phenomena. Only when there is no expression and nothing expressed can we say it is the genuine Buddhadharma.

BIG IS SMALL, SMALL IS BIG

"Subhuti, take the example of a growing body."

The Buddha said to Subhuti, "For instance, when we say the body of a person grows bigger, do you think it truly exists?" Subhuti answered, "Bhagavan, although you said the body of a person grows bigger, in fact, it is precisely because there is no bigger body that it is a bigger body." Kamalashila said that here the simile of a growing body illustrates that wisdom increases from the first bhumi of bodhisattvas until buddhahood, when it is perfect. Within the conventional, there are bigger and smaller bodies as well as sharp and dull intelligences. But at the ultimate level, these differences are untenable, and only when there is no big body is it a big body.

The *Shurangama Sutra* also said, "One is countless, countless is one. Small is big, big is small." From a conventional perspective, this statement is quite contradictory, it is impossible that small is big or big is small; however, the statement is tenable from the view that all phenomena are of no essence. For example, I dreamed of having a gigantic body, but this giant body was not a real giant body because the body in a dream is insubstantial. Similarly, the increase of a bodhisattva's wisdom is also untenable. Though attainment from the first to the tenth bhumi exists conventionally, ultimately it is unfindable.

There are many similes in the *Diamond Cutter Sutra* whose connotations cannot be revealed without examination. Here, the bigger body is analogous to the wisdom of the Buddha, while the smaller body is likened to the wisdom of bodhisattvas. In order to have a bigger body, a small body is prerequisite; similarly, in order to become a buddha, one must become a bodhisattva first. Without understanding these analogies, we might wonder why the sutra talks about buddhas and bodhisattvas then out of the blue jumps to bodies.

"No Characteristics" Is the Name of Bodhisattvas

As mentioned above, just as bodies grow bigger, bodhisattvas' wisdom also increases, but ultimately bodhisattvas do not exist.

"Subhuti, so it is with bodhisattvas. If they say, 'I will liberate immeasurable sentient beings,' they should not be called 'bodhisattvas.' Why? Subhuti, there is no substantial entity that is called a 'bodhisattva.' Therefore the Buddha said all phenomena are free from a self, a person, a sentient being, and a living being."

Through sutras that elucidate definitive meaning, we find that in the realization of great bodhisattvas, such as Manjushri and Maitreya, there is no attachment to the identity of a bodhisattva or to liberating sentient beings.

The *Sixth Patriarch Platform Sutra* also says, "Being free from any characteristics externally is called 'non-characteristics.'" "Non-characteristics" is also the name of bodhisattvas.

Earlier, the sutra said that all the buddhas transcend conceptions or attachment to characteristics, but here it says bodhisattvas are also free from them. Why? Because the Buddha said that all phenomena do not have a self, a person, a sentient being, or a living being.

The *Nirvana Sutra* also says, "All phenomena are lack of self." Since there is no real self, whence comes the conception of a person, a sentient being, and a living being?

Do Not Even Cling to "Adorning Buddha Fields"

"Subhuti, a bodhisattva who says I should adorn buddha fields is not a genuine bodhisattva. Why? The Tathagata said to adorn buddha fields does not adorn so it is called 'to adorn.'"

Within the conventional, bodhisattvas have to adorn buddha fields. The *Ornament of Clear Realization* says, "Bodhisattvas at the three pure bhumis (the eighth to the tenth bhumis) must first adorn and purify their future buddha fields."

The *Avatamsaka Sutra* and the *Mahavairocana Tantra* mention the lotus treasure world ocean; the *Gandavyuha Sutra*, or the *Excellent Manifestation Sutra*, depicts the inexhaustible sublimeness of the Gandavyuha world. The *Infinite Life Sutra* (*Sukhavativyuhah Sutra*) elucidates that through his inconceivable aspiration, Buddha Amitabha adorned the Pure Land of Great Bliss. The Shambhala world, the Copper-Colored Auspicious Mountain of Padmasambhava, and so forth have also been perceived by many great masters of Tibetan Buddhism.

These pure fields do exist within the conventional, but if a bodhisattva grasps at them, this bodhisattva is not a real bodhisattva. Why is that? Because these sublime pure lands do not exist inherently but only as emanations of pure mind. As the *Vimalakirti Sutra* says, "As the mind is pure, the buddha field is pure."

Since to adorn buddha fields exists within the conventional but does not exist when closely scrutinized, is it contradictory? No, it is not. In *Beacon of Certainty*, Mipham Rinpoche said, "It appears contradictory." In the eyes of ordinary people, conventional truth and ultimate truth appear contradictory, but they are not. Conventionally, it is to adorn buddha fields, but if we hold it to be inherently existent, it is not to adorn buddha fields anymore. Analogously, adorned buddha fields can appear in a mirror, but if the buddha fields truly exist, they could not be reflected in a mirror. It is because all phenomena lack inherent existence that they are able to appear in a mirror. This nature can be applied to all phenomena at both the conventional and ultimate levels.

SELF-CLINGING IS THE ROOT CAUSE OF CYCLIC EXISTENCE

"Subhuti, a bodhisattva who realizes selflessness would be called a genuine bodhisattva by the Tathagata."

As Mahayana practitioners, if we don't realize the emptiness of selflessness, we cannot even become listeners and self-realized buddhas, let alone great bodhisattvas. From the view of the Great Vehicle, or Nyingmapa, the attainment of shravakas requires at least realizing the selflessness of people.

Bodhisattva Nagarjuna said, "Those who have the wisdom of selflessness have the real view, those who have the wisdom of selflessness are wondrous." People who have the wisdom of selflessness appear the same as ordinary people, but their inner state is indescribable and exceedingly marvelous. If one had not realized the emptiness of selflessness, one should never be called a "bodhisattva" or "accomplisher."

Then what is "self"? The *Nirvana Sutra* says, "If a phenomenon is real, true, permanent, independent, reliable, unchanging by nature, then it can be called 'self.'" That is to say, when clinging to a "self" in relation to any phenomenon, one believes that this phenomenon is real, true, everlasting, dependable, and not empty by nature. Such attachment is the root cause of repeated death and birth in cyclic existence.

Therefore we must ensure that we realize the emptiness of selflessness. Otherwise, no matter the kind of Dharma we practice, we will never reach noble attainment. Here the passage emphasizes that without realizing selflessness, there is no way to become bodhisattvas. According to other scriptures, even the noble attainment of the Basic Vehicle would be impossible. As said in the *Sutra of Perfect Enlightenment*, "Though one has diligently practiced for eons, since this kind of practice is still called 'conditioned,' there is no chance to reach noble attainment."

18. One Body, All Visions

"Subhuti, what do you think? Does the Tathagata have flesh eyes?"
"It is so, Bhagavan. The Tathagata has flesh eyes."
"Subhuti, what do you think? Does the Tathagata have god eyes?"
"It is so, Bhagavan. The Tathagata has god eyes."
"Subhuti, what do you think? Does the Tathagata have wisdom eyes?"
"It is so, Bhagavan. The Tathagata has wisdom eyes."
"Subhuti, what do you think? Does the Tathagata have Dharma eyes?"
"It is so, Bhagavan. The Tathagata has Dharma eyes."
"Subhuti, what do you think? Does the Tathagata have Buddha eyes?"
"It is so, Bhagavan. The Tathagata has Buddha eyes."

IN ORDER to draw attention to the tone and connotations of this conversation, the questions were raised separately. A concise version could have been simply: "Subhuti, what do you think? Does the Tathagata have the five eyes?" "It is so, Bhagavan. The Tathagata has the five eyes." That's it.

As for "the five eyes," I have read a few explanations of this phrase in commentaries on the *Diamond Cutter Sutra*. Many people may not have figured out the meaning, so they often stray from the topic to avoid giving straightforward explanation. I really hope that when we study and especially teach the Dharma, there is no irrelevant talk when you do not understand something.

Moreover, it is better to cite scriptural authority when teaching the Dharma. This is a major attribute of Tibetan Buddhism. Of course, your scriptural authority must be used appropriately at suitable places; it is unacceptable to quote any authority at random. I notice that a number of people teach the Dharma not as rigorously as the great masters of the past;

whether they understand or not, they dare to teach in their own way, and their books and videos are everywhere. This is indeed not good.

The five eyes have not been mentioned in the scriptures of the Basic Vehicle, including Abhidharma of the Basic Vehicle. The Sakyapa master Koringpa said, "The six clairvoyances can be attained by the practitioners of the Basic Vehicle; the five eyes can only be acquired by the noble beings of the Great Vehicle." The sutra also said, "In order to obtain the five eyes, one must diligently practice the six perfections."

The causes, functions, ranges, and essence of the five eyes have been elaborated in the *Ornament of Clear Realization* and the Mahayana Abhidharma. In the *Manjushri-Nama-Samgiti* and the *Cakrasamvara Tantra*, it says that the excellent qualities of the Buddha are infinite and boundless and his six sensory faculties are mutually functional: any part of his body is able to perceive all objects. However, this part of the root text is only to explain the five eyes of the Buddha.

Flesh eyes

Flesh eyes can be obtained on the path of accumulation. This has resulted from making lamp offerings and engaging in meditation in previous lifetimes. Flesh eyes can perceive all sorts of gross and subtle forms within a hundred leagues up to the entire three-thousandfold universe.

Historically there were a number of great accomplishers who obtained flesh eyes. *The Words of My Perfect Teacher* records that in order to propagate the genuine Dharma, King Trisong Detsen decided to build temples. Needing to find a suitable lama to purify the land, he went to see his teacher Nyang Tingdzin Zangpo. Through his flesh eyes, the teacher found that in eastern India there lived a Khenchen Shantarakshita who was suitable to take on this role. So he informed the king, who invited Khenchen to perform the ceremony to purify the land for building temples.

God eyes

God eyes can only be possessed on the path of preparation or above. This results from virtuous practices with contamination or the six perfections, like meditation. God eyes can perceive past and future lives as well as the future rebirth location of all sentient beings of the ten directions, including hell beings and hungry ghosts. As we know, there are some yogis and sky walkers who can reveal the past and future lives of people. Some of them do possess god eyes, though some have only clairvoyance similar to god eyes.

Gateway to Knowledge also talks about god eyes, though slightly differently: "The excellence of god eyes is to perceive boundless forms."

Wisdom eyes

Wisdom eyes can be obtained when bodhisattvas of the first to the tenth bhumis enter meditative concentration. This results from virtuous practices without contamination and practicing the six perfections. Wisdom eyes are able to perceive the ultimate nature or the essence of all phenomena as they are.

It is worth mentioning that in our everyday life we often use the term "wisdom eyes" or "eyes of wisdom" to emphasize the importance of wisdom for us to "see" the truth. This common usage is different from what the sutra means by "wisdom eyes," so you need to distinguish the term according to the context.

Dharma eyes

Dharma eyes can be possessed when bodhisattvas of the first to the tenth bhumis are not in their meditative concentration. This results from virtuous practices without contamination and practicing the six perfections. Dharma eyes can realize the genuine meaning of the scripture teaching and the teaching of realization, as well as find out the capacity level of those equal or inferior to oneself. For instance, a bodhisattva at the second bhumi is able to identify the capacities of those below the first bhumi but unable to acquire the state of those above.

Buddha eyes

Buddha eyes can only be possessed in buddhahood, as a result of accumulating both merit and wisdom. Buddha eyes are the wisdom of omniscience and suchness, thoroughly perceiving the conventional and ultimate nature of all phenomena. The spectrum is vast, boundless, and inconceivable. The *Commentary on the Ornament of Clear Realization* says that bodhisattvas at the first to the tenth bhumis can obtain approximate Buddha eyes.

In regard to the excellence of the five eyes, the Sixth Patriarch gave a different explanation in the *Oral Teaching on the Diamond Cutter Sutra*. The lay practitioner Jiang Weinong has a detailed elaboration on the five eyes that slightly differs from mine but might be popular in Chinese Buddhism.

Through this introduction to the five eyes, we should understand that the Buddha has the complete excellence of the five eyes, so he can directly perceive the primordial nature free from the four extremes, and the eight types of mental fabrications at the ultimate level, and each and every thought of every sentient being within the conventional without missing anything.

NOTHING IN THIS WORLD COULD BE HIDDEN FROM THE BUDDHA

"Subhuti, what do you think? Would all the sand grains in the Ganges River be said to be sand by the Buddha?"
  "It is so, Bhagavan. The Tathagata said they are sand."

These two lines can also be found in the translation by Xuan Zang but not in the Tibetan edition or in Yi Jing's translation. It seems irrelevant to discuss the connotations of this passage; the literal meaning is sufficient for our understanding.

"Subhuti, what do you think? If there were Ganges rivers as many as the number of sand grains in the Ganges River, would buddha fields that are the same number as the sand grains of all the Ganges rivers be a great many?"
  "A great many, Bhagavan."

Buddha fields
Usually, one buddha would devote himself to taming sentient begins in one three-thousandfold universe, which includes countless small universes.

Great many
In Kumarajiva's translation "great many" is said only once, whereas in the Tibetan edition it is repeated one more time, and in Xuan Zang's translation the phrasing is: "It is so, Bhagavan, it is so, Sugata."
  The Buddha told Subhuti, "In such countless fields, the Tathagata knows the potential, capacity, and intention of each individual." The Buddha pos-

sesses extraordinary wisdom that even arhats cannot measure. The Buddha can directly perceive the capacity of every sentient being in buddha fields as many as the number of sand grains in the Ganges River. Such excellent quality is unimaginable.

The *Mysterious Inconceivable Sutra* says, "The ocean of merit of all the buddhas cannot be described in countless eons." The merit of all the buddhas is as vast as oceans; even if one spent immeasurable eons, one still could not finish recounting their merit.

In general, the Buddha has inconceivable merit, which is especially unique in knowing the capacity of sentient beings. As the *Aspiration to Be Born in Dewachen* says, "In the six sessions of day and night, the Buddha looks upon sentient beings with compassionate eyes, clearly knows any thought arising in their mind, and distinctly hears all the languages from their mouth."

In *The Introduction to the Middle Way*, when the "ten powers" are explained, it also mentions that the Buddha has the "wisdom power of knowing the capacity of all sentient beings," and that through "his wisdom power of knowing the inclination of all sentient beings," he thoroughly understands the different inclination of all sentient beings, such as the disposition of entering the Basic Vehicle or the Great Vehicle and the propensity of being born in the higher or lower realms.

Therefore even the least bit of the Buddha's merit is inconceivable. In *In Praise of the Three Bodies*, Nagarjuna praised the inexhaustible merit of the body, speech, and mind of the Buddha, especially the merit of his mind.

THE NATURE OF MIND IS LUMINOSITY

"Why? The Tathagata said, all minds are not minds, so they are called 'minds.'"

When analyzed at the ultimate level, deluded mind does not exist, neither does luminous mind. The *Eight Thousand Verses on Prajna* says, "Mind is absent of mind, the nature of mind is luminosity." There is no mind in the nature of mind, the nature of mind is luminosity—the essence of basic space (dharmadhatu), free from all mental fabrications.

Why is it said that all minds are not minds? Because the existence of mind can only be conceded within the conventional; at the ultimate level, it is unfindable. This is also the nature of all phenomena.

When teaching *The Heart Essence of Lama* in the past, our teacher H. H. Jigme Phuntsok Rinpoche elaborated extensively on why mind is unfindable. He explained it clearly with pith instructions, while the *Diamond Cutter Sutra* elucidates the unfindability of the mind with the words of the Buddha.

When we began to study the *Diamond Cutter Sutra* this time, some people suggested that I explain it from the perspective of the Great Perfection. I know the principles of the Great Perfection can fit this sutra very well, and if we refer to *The Treasure of Dharmadhatu* and *The Treasure of Ultimate Reality* along with the sutra, you can more easily understand the ultimate meaning of this sutra. However, I was hesitant to use the terms and theories of the Great Perfection because the *Diamond Cutter Sutra* is a scripture of the Sutrayana, so when my explanation is transcribed and published, people without empowerment may read it without restrictions. If we were to put "please do not read this book if you have no empowerment of the Great Perfection," such a restriction sounds weird and would limit the teaching to a select audience. So I decided to not teach the *Diamond Cutter Sutra* according to the theories of the Great Perfection.

Nevertheless, I would like to point out that the meaning of these few lines aligns very well with "refuting the existence of mind," or more vividly and loyally to its original expression, "destroy the house of mind," in the Great Perfection. The two differ only in their choice of words.

PAST, PRESENT, AND FUTURE ARE ONLY DELUSION

"Why? Subhuti, past mind is unfindable, present mind is unfindable, future mind is unfindable."

In *The Trilogy of Finding Comfort and Ease*, Venerable Longchenpa often says that past mind is no different from dreams of yesterday. The mind of the previous instant does not leave the least trace in the present, but only memory, which is not the essence of the past mind. If the essence of the past mind were to remain until now, it would have the fault of being permanent. Present mind is also unfindable. As for this clear and luminous mind at present, if we examine its color, whereabouts, and shape, we can conclude it does not exist. Future mind has not yet arisen, it has no essence at all. If a non-arising phenomenon can be found, then nonexistent phenomena, such as the sons of barren women, must also be found.

According to the pith instructions in Vajrayana, when we say past mind is unfindable, we should seek the source of mind; when we say present mind is unfindable, we should look for its whereabouts; when we say future mind is unfindable, we should find where it moves to. In general, here "unfindable" is used as the reason to examine the nature of mind. Not only is the nature of mind unfindable, but no phenomenon is findable, because all phenomena are the work of mind, and when mind is unfindable, the nature of all phenomena is also unfindable.

Therefore it is crucial to place our mind in the clear and luminous state that is free of conceptual thoughts. The *Sixth Patriarch Platform Sutra* says, "No conceptual thoughts arising is called 'sitting'; being aware of the immutable nature is called 'meditation.'" Genuine sitting meditation is to truly realize the nature of mind, which is neither coming nor going. The minds of the three times are unfindable. When I read this line, I often feel its connotation is so supreme that it is no different from the Great Perfection. Therefore we should always examine our mind. It contains profound pith instruction within!

Historically many people recognized the nature of mind through such examination. In Chinese Buddhism there was the Chan master Xuan Jian. He became a monk in childhood and was able to give Dharma teachings when very young; since he had a unique understanding of the *Diamond Cutter Sutra*, and his surname was Zhou, he was called "Diamond Zhou." Later on he believed that he had achieved some realization and had been versed in the Dharma. When he heard that the Chan tradition, which advocated directly pointing out the nature of mind and reaching buddhahood by recognizing it, was flourishing in southern China, a thought occurred to him: "My wisdom is second to none. Now there are demons spreading wrong views in the south. I have a responsibility to check it out and subjugate those demons." So he went south with a bag containing the *Commentary on the Diamond Cutter Sutra: Green Dragon*, composed by himself.

One day on his way, he stopped at a booth to buy some dim sum (dumplings). Out of curiosity, the granny selling the dim sum said to him, "Young Master, your bag looks very heavy, what's in it?"

"The *Commentary on the Diamond Cutter Sutra*."

"Do you understand it?"

"Not only do I understand it, I have taught it for years."

"Great! I have a question for you. If you can answer it, I would like to offer you some dim sum for free; however, if you cannot answer it, please buy the dim sum elsewhere. OK?"

"No problem!"

"The *Diamond Cutter Sutra* says, 'Past mind is unfindable, present mind is unfindable, future mind is unfindable.' Which sum (mind) do you dim (point to)?"[10]

Unable to utter a word, the young master had to resume his journey without having the dim sum. However, his mind dwelled on this question.

Finally, he arrived at the temple of Chan master Long Tan that night. After paying a brief visit with the old master, he had to leave. Finding it dark outside, he went back to ask for lighting. Master Long Tan lit a candle and handed it to him.

Just when he was about to grab the candle, but still pondering that granny's question, the old master suddenly blew out that candle. Hearing the sound "puh," the young master achieved enlightenment at that very moment.

19. Pervasive Liberation in Dharmadhatu

ATTACHMENT STEALS ALMOST ALL THE MERIT FROM GENEROSITY

"Subhuti, what do you think? If someone gives away the seven jewels that fill up the entire three-thousandfold universe, through these causes and conditions, would this person attain great merit?"

"Yes, it would be so, Bhagavan. Through these causes and conditions, this person would attain great merit."

PUTTING ASIDE the seven jewels that fill the three-thousandfold universe, as the sutra said, even when making an offering of a fresh flower or a cup of clean water to the supreme merit field, the merit would be inconceivable.

"Subhuti, if merit has substantial essence, the Tathagata would not say the merit would be great. It is because merit does not exist that the Tathagata said the merit is great."

This statement has been connected with the previous statement by a question that links the two. Earlier in the text, it says "past mind is unfindable, present mind is unfindable, and future mind is unfindable." Some people might take to heart the doubt that is raised by the question, "Since the minds of the three times are unfindable, wouldn't the accumulation of merit be in vain?" The answer to this question is negative. Although the essence of mind is unfindable, within the conventional, accumulating merit through practicing generosity would never be in vain, and this merit would not be exhausted until achieving buddhahood.

As we all know, sutras have introduced different practices for Great Vehicle followers. Generosity is one of the skillful means most suitable for beginners. Through it, one can swiftly accumulate merit, purify obscurations, and finally attain supreme buddhahood. Then if someone gives away the seven jewels that fill the three-thousandfold universe, would the merit be great? Subhuti completely understood the secret meaning of the Buddha, so he replied that the merit would be immense.

Why is the merit so immense? Because it is empty. As said in *The Fundamental Wisdom of the Middle Way*, "Any phenomenon that arises from causes and conditions, I say it is empty by nature." Generosity is a phenomenon that arises from causes and conditions, so its essence is empty, and because it is insubstantial, it can create immense merit.

Obviously, as ordinary people who have not yet realized emptiness, we might find it difficult to comprehend this reason. Only when we have a firm certainty on emptiness, understanding that all phenomena do not have even a sesame-seed bit of true existence, can we find its rationality.

If merit truly exists, the Tathagata would never say that practicing generosity can create immense merit. As mentioned earlier, a bodhisattva should give rise to bodhichitta without fixating on form, sound, smell, taste, touch, or dharma—should give rise to bodhichitta without fixating on anything. Only by practicing generosity without fixating on any characteristics can immense merit arise; practicing generosity with attachment creates almost no merit.

In the past, Emperor Wu of Liang once asked Master Dharma, "Since my enthronement, I have done countless virtues for the Three Jewels, such as building buddha statues, printing sutras, and offering to the sangha. Have I attained great merit?"

Master Dharma replied, "No merit." Very unhappy to hear this, Emperor Wu of Liang went off in a huff.

Why did Master Dharma reply in this way? Emperor Wu of Liang believed that merit truly exists, but if he understood that the essence of virtue is empty by nature, he would not have thought he was marvelous. Therefore attachment to true existence is a great obstacle. We should eliminate it. As said in the wisdom chapter of *Guide to the Bodhisattva's Way of Life*, "We should not eliminate what we hear, feel, and know. It is our attachment to true existence, the cause of suffering, that should be eliminated."

As we can see, what we need to get rid of is not phenomena themselves but our attachment to phenomena because that is the cause of the suffering of sentient beings, the cause of cyclic existence.

In general, if phenomena truly exist, there would be no merit arising

from them. It is precisely because all phenomena are dependently origi-
nated and empty by nature, like dreams and illusions, that merit is able to
arise when causes and conditions are present.

20. Transcend Form and Characteristics

RUPAKAYA IS DHARMAKAYA, DHARMAKAYA IS RUPAKAYA

"Subhuti, what do you think? Can one meet the Buddha through his form body?"

"No, Bhagavan. The Tathagata should not be met through form body. Why? The Tathagata said when attaining the form body, it is not attaining the form body; only when it is not form body is it form body."

YOU HAVE no doubt already noticed that the nature of all phenomena has often been expounded in this sutra by integrating both ultimate and conventional truths. If one scrutinizes closely, one can find the links between topics that are covered earlier and later.

Earlier, it was explained from the merit aspect that through accumulating merit, the form body, or rupakaya, can be attained; here, it is explained from the wisdom aspect that the accumulation of wisdom results in the emergence of dharmakaya. These are the special connections between cause and effect.

As Bodhisattva Nagarjuna said in the *Sixty Stanzas on Reasoning*, "By this merit that I dedicate to all sentient beings, may their accumulation of merit and wisdom increase, and may they attain the two bodies."

Some people might ask, "Does rupakaya arising from merit truly exist?" It does not. We say that merit can produce form body, but this can only be conceded within the conventional. From the view of the ultimate truth, form body and merit are free from mental fabrication. These two are neither independent nor linked by the duality of the producer and the produced. Therefore, rupakaya is dharmakaya, dharmakaya is rupakaya.

As said in the *Awakening of Faith in the Mahayana*, "It is because truth body is form body that all forms can appear." Truth body is actually form body, and different forms can appear from form body.

People who cannot comprehend the Great Vehicle sutras might think this is contradictory, but all the scriptures with definitive meaning present such views. The form body of the Tathagata is not a form body but rather an appearance that is empty by nature, free from fabrication, and pervasively luminous.

The famous line in the *Heart Sutra*, "form is emptiness, emptiness is form," also shares the same principle.

THE TRUE BODY OF THE TATHAGATA IS AN UNCONDITIONED PHENOMENON

Excellent major and minor marks are part of rupakaya. Without rupakaya, can the excellent marks of the Buddha exist? They cannot exist either.

"Subhuti, what do you think? Can one see the Tathagata through seeing his excellent marks?"

"No, Bhagavan. One cannot see the Tathagata through seeing his excellent marks."

Within the conventional, when the Buddha was in this world, many sentient beings were able to see his thirty-two excellent major marks. As said in the *Avatamsaka Sutra*, "When reaching buddhahood, one would possess the thirty-two major marks and be revered by gods, humans, yakshas, nagas, and so forth." But in fact, the form body of the Tathagata does not have any truly existent marks; the thirty-two major marks are only a symbol of achieving buddhahood and are not truly existent. Therefore it is untenable to think one can see the Tathagata through seeing his physical marks.

The buddha statue is an expedient icon for blessing; it has inconceivable merit, but not in an ultimate sense. As said in *Guide to the Bodhisattva's Way of Life*, "When others destroy buddha statues or stupas, do not let hatred arise toward them, because buddha statues and stupas do not have feelings." After all, the true body of the Tathagata is an unconditioned phenomenon. Unconditioned phenomena cannot be burned by fire or smashed by tools. From the view of Vajrayana, buddha statues and stupas are nondefinitive and illusory matrices.

Saying this does not mean we should give up revering buddha statues. People with immature wisdom often go to extremes, either too far left or too far right, and commit grave misdeeds that lead to the lower realms.

This is also why the teachings of the Great Vehicle can only be given before Dharma vessels but never before unqualified Dharma receivers.

Many people are unable to accept this view and believe that only with their nose and two eyes can the existence of the Buddha be confirmed. In fact, only when one reaches enlightenment can one actually see the Buddha. In the Chan tradition it has always been said recognizing the nature of mind is also recognizing the Buddha; however, this Buddha does not have a face or marks!

"Why? The Tathagata said possessing excellent marks is not possessing excellent marks, so it is called 'possessing excellent marks.'"

Ordinary people believe the Tathagata should either possess excellent marks or not possess excellent marks. There are no other possibilities. However, the actual characteristics of the Tathagata are inconceivable and inexpressible.

Analogously, when my body is reflected in a mirror, you cannot find a real me in the mirror, but you cannot say my reflection in the mirror has nothing to do with me. Therefore all characteristics are not ultimate reality, and the state of the Tathagata cannot be imagined by our conceptual thoughts.

21. Not What Has Been Said

SILENCE IS TO TEACH, TO TEACH IS SILENCE

"Subhuti, you should not say the Tathagata has the thought: 'I have Dharma to teach.' You should also give up thinking this. Why? If someone says the Tathagata has Dharma to teach, they have already slandered the Buddha and failed to understand what I said."

PEOPLE UNFAMILIAR with the Great Vehicle, especially those who do not know the secret meaning of the Great Vehicle, might find this passage difficult to accept. It is so obvious that the Buddha had turned the wheel of Dharma three times, presented 84,000 teachings, and said that he taught this and that at such and such time.

Why is the obvious negated here? And why did Buddha go so far as to assert that if you say the Buddha taught the Dharma, you are deliberately maligning the Buddhadharma? This is indeed puzzling.

In fact, before the confused sensory consciousness of sentient beings, countless buddhas of the past have each taught a different variety of Buddhadharma. As said in the *Lotus Sutra*, "The Buddha said in past times that countless late buddhas had taught this Dharma while abiding in skillful means." But this statement is tenable only within the conventional; in ultimate reality, the one who turns the wheel of Dharma does not truly exist, the wheel of Dharma that was turned does not truly exist, and the enlightened activities of liberating sentient beings through turning the wheel of Dharma does not truly exist.

The nature of all phenomena is emptiness. Other than teaching emptiness, the Buddha never taught any Dharma. All the Dharma that has been taught is only a façade within the conventional and does not exist at the ultimate level.

At the conventional level, we cannot deny that the illusory Bhagavan had turned the illusory wheel of Dharma three times and liberated countless illusory sentient beings. Here, this is not refuted. What the sutra tries to convey is that in the nature of ultimate reality, there is no such event as Buddha Shakyamuni turning the wheel of Dharma to liberate sentient beings.

In the *Jewel Power Sutra*, Bodhisattva Manjushri said to the Buddha, "Whoever teaches the Buddhadharma relying on terms and languages, these Buddhadharma transcend all characteristics and do not truly exist."

The *Awakening Song* also says, "Silence is to teach, to teach is silence." The Buddha has never taught any Dharma. Only through silence, not uttering a single word, can the Buddha present the ultimate reality."

THE BUDDHA HAS NEVER UTTERED ONE SINGLE WORD OF BUDDHADHARMA

"Subhuti, the teacher has no Dharma to teach, so it is said 'to teach the Dharma.'"

After sufficient mastery to distinguish the conventional truth from the ultimate truth, you will realize that all the subjects covered so far in this sutra are very much the same, only presented from different aspects.

As far as the nature of ultimate reality is concerned, the Buddha constantly abides in the emptiness of the three spheres, completely transcending conceptual thoughts like, "I will liberate sentient beings by turning the wheel of Dharma." He only manifested as teaching the Dharma before confused sentient beings in order to crush their dreamlike self-clinging.

The *Golden Light Sutra* says, "It has never occurred to the Buddha, 'I need to present the Dharma of the twelve categories in order to benefit sentient beings.'" Since the Buddha never thought of teaching the sutras of the twelve categories nor intended to benefit sentient beings, the adept who teaches the Dharma is untenable, as the Dharma that has been taught does not truly exist in ultimate reality.

In brief, since what has been taught and who is able to teach do not exist, we can say the Tathagata has no Dharma to teach. The *Parinirvana Sutra* also says, "Since I reached buddhahood until I entered parinirvana, I have never uttered a single word of Buddhadharma." In a nutshell, the teacher and what has been taught do not exist in ultimate reality. However, within the conventional it is tenable to concede that in order to counteract the 84,000 afflictive emotions of sentient beings, the Buddha taught 84,000 types of Buddhadharma.

At that time, Venerable Subhuti asked the Buddha, "Bhagavan, in the future, after a great number of sentient beings hear this Dharma, will they gain faith?"

The Buddha said, "Subhuti, sentient beings are neither sentient beings nor non-sentient beings. Why? Subhuti, as for sentient beings, the Tathagata said 'are not sentient beings but are named sentient beings.'"

Earlier in this sutra, the Buddha mentioned that with his wisdom eyes he is able to clearly perceive the future when sentient beings gain great faith after they listen to and contemplate the *Diamond Cutter Sutra*. This can be agreed on within the conventional; however, here the answer is, those who will gain faith in the future do not exist at all. Why is that so? Within the conventional we can concede that imputed illusory sentient beings exist, but in ultimate reality the least trace of their existence cannot be established.

The *King of Meditative Concentration* says, "Just as people who seek the core of a fresh plantain tree cannot find anything substantial from the inside out, so is the nature of all phenomena." Sentient beings are like plantain trees: without examination they seem to exist solidly, but with scrutiny we find they do not have even the tiniest bit of essence."

If this is the case, then in the ultimate reality, gaining faith in this sutra through listening and reflecting on it does not exist, and the immense merit of revering, paying homage to, chanting, and upholding this sutra also does not exist.

22. No Dharma to Attain

Subhuti asked the Buddha, "Bhagavan, the Buddha attained the perfect, unsurpassable enlightenment, but actually, has he attained nothing?"

The Buddha said, "Thus it is, thus it is. Subhuti, because I did not attain anything when I attained the perfect, unsurpassable enlightenment, it is said I have attained the perfect, unsurpassable enlightenment."

ULTIMATE NIRVANA is not attainable. As Bodhisattva Nagarjuna said in his *Fundamental Wisdom of the Middle Way*:

Neither abandoning nor attaining,
neither nihilism nor everlasting,
neither arising nor ceasing,
that is the so-called nirvana.

This subject was covered earlier. However, Kamalashila said this subject was covered earlier from the "view" of the path of learning (the first to the tenth bhumis of bodhisattvas), whereas here it is addressed again in regard to the merit of the path of no more learning (buddhahood).

In general, in ultimate reality, the Tathagata has attained nothing.

23. Purifying Mind and Cultivating Virtue

WHAT IS THE PERFECT, UNSURPASSABLE ENLIGHTENMENT?

"Moreover, Subhuti, when all phenomena are equal and transcend superior or inferior, it is the perfect, unsurpassable enlightenment."

AS SAID in the *Avatamsaka Sutra*, "By nature, all buddhas and I are equal." In *On the Five Stages* Nagarjuna also said, "Appearance and emptiness are (perceived as) distinctive attributes; whenever they are (perceived) as oneness, it is called the union (the same as equality)." Therefore, in the ultimate reality, buddhas are no different from sentient beings, and hells and nirvana are equal by nature.

WISDOM AND COMPASSION ARE INSEPARABLE

"Those who transcend the conceptions of a self, a person, a sentient being, and a living being can attain the perfect, unsurpassable enlightenment through practicing virtuous Dharma."

First and foremost we must accumulate merit and purify obscurations at our causal stage. However, in this course we must also try to diminish our attachment to inherent existence. If we practice diligently while clinging strongly to the true existence of sentient beings and buddhas, we will be unable to reach the ultimate attainment of buddhahood.

As said in the *Sixth Patriarch Platform Sutra*, "This mind is pure originally, so it does not distinguish between what to adopt and what to abandon." Therefore our mind needs to be pure; only when transcending the self of people and the self of phenomena as well as the four conceptions can we attain the unsurpassable buddhahood. If we hold virtuous deeds and accumulations to be truly existent, we will attain the karmic effect only as humans or gods but fail to reach enlightenment.

People who have not comprehended emptiness often hold amassing accumulations and attaining buddhahood to be truly existent; they strongly believe their virtuous deeds would never exhaust in any circumstances. Although we concede that the karmic law of cause and effect is unerring within the conventional, in ultimate reality any phenomenon has never arisen and is great emptiness. There is no true buddhahood to attain. As said in the *Shurangama Sutra*, "In the final analysis, perfect enlightenment is unattainable."

After hearing the *Diamond Cutter Sutra*, we should lessen our strong attachment to the inherent existence of virtuous roots, the Tathagata, and so forth. If this attachment, the root cause of cyclic existence, cannot be eradicated, buddhahood is unreachable. The Buddha did concede that practicing virtue creates merit, but if the practice has not been imbued with the emptiness of the three spheres, it would not be the ultimate cause for liberation. Therefore wisdom and compassion are inseparable. Whatever we practice, it is important to be imbued with the view of emptiness.

In *Luminous Essence*, Mipham Rinpoche also examined the eleven topics of Vajrayana with the view of the Great Perfection. No matter whether it is the view or it is meditative concentration, there must be the great emptiness transcending all mental fabrication, which is also the ultimate goal of our practice.

DOES GIVING UP ATTACHMENT MEAN GIVING UP EVERYTHING?

"Subhuti, the Tathagata said the so-called virtuous Dharma is not virtuous Dharma, so it is virtuous Dharma."

There are a great variety of virtuous Dharmas. As for the virtuous Dharmas that lead to merit, there are ten kinds; and for virtuous Dharmas that lead to liberation, there are thirty-seven factors of enlightenment and so forth. All these virtuous Dharmas exist like illusions and dreams within the conventional, but ultimately, virtuous Dharmas are only an expedient skillful means.

The Sixth Patriarch said, "Neither think of virtue nor think of nonvirtue," and "When engaging in any virtuous Dharma, if one wishes for the reward, it is non-virtuous Dharma." As a result, at the conventional level, practicing virtue leads to liberation and brings happiness to sentient beings, but ultimately, virtuous Dharma does not exist at all.

It is easy for the practitioners of the Great Vehicle to understand this view, but for many followers of the Basic Vehicle it is unfathomable. Although they have strong faith in and a fortunate connection with the Buddha, their attachment toward the inherent existence of phenomena is so strong that they always believe the body of the Buddha is solid and unchangeable and that buddhahood exists intrinsically.

To refute this view, the Chan monk Mahayana said, "No matter if it is a black dog or a white dog, when the dog bites someone, the blood shed will be red. Similarly, no matter if it is virtuous Dharma or non-virtuous Dharma, as long as you attach to it, that is the cause for samsara."

Some people's practice is so diligent, their motivation so pure, their prostration, offering, and giving away are never interrupted; but it is a shame that they have never studied the teachings on emptiness and believe that buddhahood exists inherently.

Although it is indeed difficult for ordinary beings to realize emptiness, while accumulating merit and purifying obscuration at the causal stage, it is necessary to gradually get rid of our attachment toward the ground, path, and fruition.

Obviously to get rid of attachment does not mean to give up practicing virtuous Dharma. People with little wisdom often fall into extremes, thinking that no attachment means giving up everything. With this wrong view they deny the karmic law of cause and effect and finally fall into the frightful wrong view of nihilism.

Therefore, as wrong views pervade the world these days, do your best to protect your right views and avoid being ruined by rampant wrong views that might lead you to a wrong lifestyle!

24. Incomparable Merit and Wisdom

THE INCOMPARABLE MERIT OF UPHOLDING THE *DIAMOND CUTTER SUTRA*

THE SEVEN JEWELS are great in number, but once consumed, birth and death are still unavoidable; the four lines in the sutra are small in number, but once realized, enlightenment could be reached.

"Subhuti, if someone were to give away all the seven jewels filling up all the Mount Merus in the three-thousandfold universe, and if another person were to uphold, recite, and teach this sutra of prajnaparamita, or even a four-line verse of it, the merit created by the former would be less than one-hundredth of a thousandth or millionth of the latter, which could not even be measured or expressed with similes."

The seven jewels filling up all the Mount Merus

There are two ways to interpret this line. First, as the seven jewels covering all these Mount Merus; second, piling up the seven jewels as high as these Mount Merus.

The other day an old lady stopped me and said, "Khenpo, I really cannot understand why the *Diamond Cutter Sutra* has immense merit. Can you help me understand it?" I was in a rush and didn't give her a great answer, so now let me explain it better. On the one hand, the *Diamond Cutter Sutra* is the origin of all the buddhas of the three times; all the buddhas and bodhisattvas have relied on it to achieve accomplishment. On the other hand, if we are able to recite and uphold this sutra, we familiarize ourselves with the causes of buddhas and bodhisattvas, and in the end we will be able to attain the wisdom of the Tathagata.

As mentioned earlier, the merit of upholding this sutra far surpasses that of giving away material goods. Why is that? With regard to karmic effect, giving away material wealth brings a fortunate result only in human and god realms; at best we can become a wheel-turning monarch, Brahma, or Indra, or those who possess perfect enjoyments. But upholding and chanting this sutra can bring us the perfect, ultimate buddhahood.

From the standpoint of realization, giving away material wealth creates only virtuous roots that are easily exhausted, whereas upholding and chanting the sutra of transcendental wisdom can help us to realize emptiness and transcend the suffering ocean of samsara. Therefore the Emperor Xuan Zong of Tang said, "The seven jewels in the three-thousandfold universe are great in number, but once consumed, birth and death are still unavoidable; the four lines in the sutra are small in number, but once realized, enlightenment could be reached." There is a world of difference between the merit of these two!

Some people have made enormous donations, but if their virtuous action is not imbued with the view of emptiness, it would still have the nature of arising and ceasing, which is not the cause for liberation. However, if you could realize emptiness for even one instant, you would be able to attain enlightenment at that very moment because realizing emptiness is the root cause for enlightenment.

The *Heart Sutra* says, "Relying on prajnaparamita, the buddhas of the three times have attained the perfect, unsurpassable enlightenment."

The *Sixth Patriarch Platform Sutra* says:

> Once direct perception of prajna arises,
> all delusory thoughts will be pacified in one instant;
> once recognizing the nature of your being,
> you reach enlightenment, or even buddhahood.

As a result, the merit of material offerings is incomparable to that of upholding this sutra.

25. Liberate Nobody

"Subhuti, what do you think? You should not say that the Tathagata has the thought, 'I should liberate sentient beings.' Subhuti, give up this thought. Why? There is no sentient being that the Tathagata can liberate. If there were sentient beings that the Tathagata could liberate, the Tathagata must have the conception of a self, a person, a sentient being, and a living being."

WITHIN the conventional, practitioners should generate the unsurpassable bodhichitta to liberate sentient beings in the future. We know that buddhas of the ten directions have made this aspiration and have appeared to liberate countless sentient beings. As the *Lotus Sutra* says, "Relying on countless skillful means, all the buddhas have liberated sentient beings and guided them into the uncontaminated wisdom of the Buddha."

The Buddha's way of liberating sentient beings differs greatly from ours. We ordinary people rely on our conceptual thoughts. The Buddha's way of liberating sentient beings, as said in the *Mahasamnipata Sutra of the Moon Treasure*, falls into four categories:

1. Liberating sentient beings with Dharma: turning the wheel of Dharma of the eighty-four thousand teachings, expounding sutras of twelve sections.
2. Liberating sentient beings with body: the body of the Buddha has infinite light rays, excellent major and minor marks; sentient beings can be greatly benefited by visualizing buddhas.
3. Liberating sentient beings with clairvoyance: in the presence of sentient beings with fortunate connections, the Buddha displayed limitless clairvoyance, power, and various emanations.
4. Liberating sentient beings with names: buddhas have countless names and titles, when chanting them with one-pointed mind,

sentient beings are able to eliminate their obscurations and obtain great benefit.

As said in the *Sigalovada Sutra*, "Hearing the name of Buddha Shakyamuni, sentient beings will never fall into the lower realms." As we can see, at the conventional level the Buddha must have the aspiration and action of "I will liberate sentient beings." However, in ultimate reality the liberator and the liberated do not exist and are free from mental fabrication.

As the *Perfect Enlightenment Sutra* says, "What is the conception of a self? It is what the minds of sentient beings have realized." In their illusory appearance, about-to-be-liberated sentient beings seem to exist, but in ultimate reality there are no real sentient beings that need to be liberated.

The Sixth Patriarch also said, "In ultimate reality, sentient beings are buddhas; it would be false speech to say they need to be liberated." Therefore the root text says, "If there were sentient beings that the Tathagata could liberate, the Tathagata must have the conception of a self, a person, a sentient being, and a living being." Having these four conceptions, there is no way to reach nirvana!

What Differentiates Ordinary Beings from Noble Beings

"Subhuti, when the Tathagata said there is a self, there is not a self, but ordinary beings believe there is a self."

In Buddhist scriptures the nonexistence of a self is examined in various ways, but since ordinary people are unable to comprehend this view, they still cling strongly to this self.

What are ordinary beings? Those who have not understood the noble Dharma as it is. As said in the Mahayana *Great Treatise of the Five Aggregates*, "What is called 'the nature of various birth' (*prthag jana*)? Those who have not realized the noble Dharma." "Various birth" is an alternative name for ordinary beings; it means ordinary beings take birth in the six realms of samsara due to their various karmic effects.

Compared with noble beings, ordinary beings have the conception of a self, a person, a sentient being, and a living being, and have not yet removed the attachment to "I" and the attachment to "mine." Noble beings have completely realized selflessness and are free from the attachment to any self both theoretically and in their actual realization.

The difference between ordinary and noble beings is apparent at the conventional level, but is it reasonable to cling to this difference? The following passage addresses this issue.

GIVE UP CLINGING TO YOURSELF AS AN ORDINARY BEING

"Subhuti, ordinary beings are said by the Tathagata to not be ordinary beings."

In the meditative concentration of the fundamental wisdom of noble beings, there are no ordinary beings or non-ordinary beings. The *Vimalakirti Sutra* says, "There are neither ordinary beings nor non-ordinary beings; neither noble beings nor non-noble beings." Within the conventional, ordinary beings exist, but in ultimate truth the nature of ordinary beings is no different from the suchness of the Buddha. Since ordinary beings do not exist, neither does realizing selflessness and not realizing selflessness. Here again, please distinguish the two truths!

26. Dharmakaya Has No Marks

EACH OF THE EXCELLENT MARKS OF THE BUDDHA COMES FROM IMMEASURABLE MERIT

"Subhuti, what do you think? Can the Tathagata be met by the thirty-two marks?"

Subhuti answered, "Yes, yes. The Tathagata can be met through the thirty-two marks."

WITHIN THE CONVENTIONAL, the Buddha does have the sublime thirty-two excellent marks. In *The Precious Garland of the Middle Way*, Bodhisattva Nagarjuna elaborated how each mark arose from a corresponding merit.

The *Golden Light Sutra* says, "Bhagavan is of immense merit, of subtle and sublime excellent marks. His sublime body is ornamented with thousands of types of merit." Definitive sutras of the Great Vehicle, such as the *Tathagatagarbha Sutra*, frequently mention his excellent marks. As a result, Subhuti said, it can be conceded within the conventional that the Tathagata can be met through his thirty-two excellent marks.

THIRTY-TWO EXCELLENT MARKS

Here the Buddha had a debate with Subhuti. First, the Buddha pointed out that Subhuti's reply was not correct.

The Buddha said, "Subhuti, if the Tathagata could be met through his thirty-two excellent marks, then a wheel-turning monarch should also be the Tathagata."

This is a debate based on logical analysis. Subhuti said, "The Tathagata can be met through the thirty-two excellent marks." If we admit that the Tathagata could be met by the thirty-two excellent marks, the logical conclusion would be that "the wheel-turning monarch has become the Tathagata," which is false.

The *Jataka* relates that when Buddha Shakyamuni was born King Suddhodana invited fortune tellers to predict the baby prince's future. It was said that if he did not renounce worldly life, he would become a wheel-turning monarch, and if he renounced the mundane world, he would become a buddha. If Buddha Shakyamuni could have taken the path of a wheel-turning monarch, by inference the wheel-turning monarch could also have thirty-two excellent marks. Subhuti made a careless mistake in his reasoning and conclusions.

Based on the meaning of this passage, there are different "thirty-two excellent marks," so the marks of the Buddha and the monarch cannot be treated as the same. As said in the *Abhidharmakosha*, the thirty-two excellent marks of the Buddha are far superior to those of the wheel-turning monarch in their sublimeness, prominence, and perfection. For instance, the protrusion on the body of the Buddha is in the center of his crown, whereas the wheel-turning monarch's is slightly left or right of the center and not as sublime as the Buddha's. The thirty-two excellent marks of the Buddha are prominent, whereas the wheel-turning monarch's are not easily noticed. The excellent marks of the Buddha are perfect and flawless, whereas the wheel-turning monarch's have some minor defects.

Though both marks are called the "thirty-two excellent marks," how can the inferior thirty-two excellent marks of the wheel-turning monarch compare to those of the Buddha?

IS BURNING INCENSE AND PROSTRATING TO THE BUDDHA USEFUL?

As a response to Buddha Shakyamuni's reminder, Subhuti awakened to the truth immediately.

Subhuti told the Buddha, "Bhagavan, from my understanding of what the Buddha has said, the Tathagata cannot be seen by the thirty-two excellent marks."
Then the Bhagavan said, "If he sees me through form or seeks me by sound, this person has already entered the wrong path, unable to see the Tathagata."

> *If he sees me through form,*
> *seeks me by sound,*

this person has already entered the wrong way,
unable to see the actual face of the Tathagata.

Great masters of Tibetan Buddhism all like to quote this verse. I have the impression that it has been cited in Je Tsongkhapa's *Great Treatise of the Fundamental Wisdom of the Middle Way*, *The Introduction to the Way of the Great Vehicle* (*Theg pa chen po'i tshul la 'jug pa*) by Pandita Rongzom Chökyi Sangpo (1012–88), and *The Seven Treasures* by Venerable Longchen Rabjam, as well as some commentaries by Mipham Rinpoche.

From the perspective of dharmakaya, or emptiness, when fortunate disciples saw the sublime body and marks of the Buddha, the phenomenon was only pure dependent-arising (*paratantra-svabhava*), not the actual Buddha.

Seeking the Buddha by chanting buddha names and sutras is also not the definitive meaning of the Tathagata. The actual face of the Tathagata is neither the form seen by the eyes nor the sound heard by the ears; therefore, if one wants to meet the Tathagata through form and sound, one has already strayed from the right track.

Here the wrong path does not mean the path of demons or heretics, but rather the worldly view of clinging to form and shape. As said in the *Sixth Patriarch Platform Sutra*, "Right view is called 'supramundane'; wrong view is 'mundane.'"

As said in *The Four Hundred Stanzas on the Middle Way*, when the Buddha entered parinirvana, there were no aggregates, nor was there an imputed self that relied on aggregates. If we take the Tathagata as form arising from aggregates, we are utterly mistaken.

The Fundamental Wisdom of the Middle Way says, "Those who are heavily stained with wrong views cling to the existence of the Tathagata; although the Tathagata is peaceful by nature they believe [the Tathagata] is either existent or nonexistent." According to the ultimate view of both Vajrayana and Sutrayana, when the nature of mind is realized, that is the real Tathagata, there is no other Tathagata in physical form.

Some people explain this passage from the *Diamond Cutter Sutra* without distinguishing what is definitive and what is expedient. In fact, the interpretation would go wrong if the passage is not explained from the perspective of the ultimate truth. We need to make this clear. Otherwise, after studying the *Diamond Cutter Sutra*, those active in accumulating merit might mistakenly think burning incense and prostrating to the Buddha is meaningless because the Tathagata does not exist at all.

As we study the *Diamond Cutter Sutra*, we should learn to identify and abandon this wrong view! At the ultimate level, excellent marks do not represent the Tathagata. As the *Sutra Revealing the Nonorigination of Dharmas* (*Sarvadharmapravrttinirdesa Sutra*; Tib. *Chos thans cad 'byung ba*) says, "When there is neither Buddha nor Dharma, that is known as the great wisdom." This is said from the perspective of emptiness.

Ultimately speaking, the Tathagata is not nothingness. In the Tibetan edition there is one more verse following the previous, which also appears in the translations of Xuan Zang and Yi Jing, though it is absent in Kumarajiva's, possibly because the Sanskrit version he used does not have this verse or this verse was accidently edited out. So please add this verse when you chant the sutra:

> View the nature of the Buddha,
> the dharmakaya of the Guide.
> The nature of the dharmakaya is not what is known,
> so it cannot be comprehended.

When citing the previous verse, great masters in Tibet always add this verse as well. The verse means the essence of all the buddhas should be viewed free of mental fabrication, which is also the dharmakaya of the Guide leading all sentient beings. The dharmakaya is unconditioned phenomena, luminous and free from mental fabrication. It transcends the state of object and subject, so the conceptual thoughts of ordinary people cannot comprehend it.

As said in *Guide to the Bodhisattva's Way of Life*, "Ultimate truth is not the object of the mind; whenever the mind is the subject, its [object is] conventional." The ultimate truth is not the object of the conceptual thoughts of ordinary people. Conceptual thoughts belong to the conventional level and cannot fathom the inconceivable nature of dharma.

The *Golden Light Sutra* also says, "Even if all gods and human beings spent countless eons contemplating ultimate truth, they could not understand it."

27. Neither Nihilism nor Ceasing

EXCELLENT MARKS ARE THE RESULT OF CAUSES AND CONDITIONS

"Subhuti, if you have the thought: 'It was (not) through his excellent marks that the Tathagata attained the perfect, unsurpassable enlightenment,' give up this thinking. The Tathagata did not attain the perfect, unsurpassable enlightenment through his excellent marks."

NEITHER the Tibetan edition nor Xuan Zang's translation gives the word "not" parenthetically. According to the context, it would be more correct to delete "not" here and when chanting the sutra. However, since Kumarajiva's version contains true words of great blessing, it is OK to keep "not." I myself believe that the word was not in the original translation by Kumarajiva but was accidently added later during the course of circulation.

The excellent marks are mentioned repeatedly to emphasize that if one believes the perfect, unsurpassable enlightenment can be attained through excellent marks, you are mistaken. What is a so-called mark? The *Lankavatara Sutra* says, "As to marks, the appearances—of location, form, shape, image, and so forth—can be defined as 'marks.'"

In fact, marks only arise from causes and conditions, and any phenomenon arising from causes and conditions is an empty mark. *The Great Treatise on the Perfection of Wisdom* says, "Phenomena arising from causes and conditions are called 'empty marks.'" Therefore, if one strongly believes that the perfect, unsurpassable enlightenment can be attained through excellent marks, one would fall into the extreme of permanence and never attain the perfect, unsurpassable enlightenment.

THE TRUE REALITY IS RATHER THAN NOTHINGNESS

"Subhuti, if you have the thought, 'Those who have generated the perfect, unsurpassable bodhichitta would say all phenomena do not exist,' give up this thinking! Why? People who have generated the perfect, unsurpassable bodhichitta would never say phenomena have the characteristics of nihilism."

When examining phenomena, if we believe that all appearances do not exist, that there is mere emptiness, that is nihilism. For instance, some people claim that the karmic laws of cause and effect and of rebirth do not exist, only emptiness exists. This is an untenable position. The real meaning of "all phenomena are emptiness" is as said in the *Heart Sutra*—all phenomena are "unborn and unceasing."

If we say that it is in the nature of reality for all phenomena to cease but not arise, that view falls into the extreme of nihilism, and even the Buddha is unable to liberate us. As said in *The Fundamental Wisdom of the Middle Way*, "The emptiness taught by the Conqueror transcends all views. If a person clings to a view of emptiness, he could not be liberated by any buddha."

If one practices from the standpoint of nihilism (mere emptiness), one would be born in the formless realm where sentient beings abide in the meditative concentration of one object and after death head to the next life of pervasive suffering, unable to transcend samsara. Venerable Longchen Rabjam criticized this view in *Finding Comfort and Ease in the Nature of Mind*, saying those who hold this view belong with the heretics.

28. No Attaining, No Clinging

Is Dharma Study Only for Dispelling Conflictive Emotions?

"Subhuti, if a bodhisattva has given away the seven jewels filling up as many universes as the number of the sand grains in the Ganges River, and another person has understood that all phenomena are selfless and has attained the tolerance of non-arising, the merit of the latter far surpasses that of the former."

As we have seen, the merit of making offerings or giving is immense. However, if one has gained certainty regarding the truth of selflessness by listening, reflecting, and meditating, the merit is even more inconceivable.

As we know, if our mind is impure, our virtuous giving does not necessarily create great merit. However, after listening, reflecting, and meditating, even if we practice emptiness for just one instant and gain irreversible certainty regarding selflessness, or non-arising, the merit would be indescribable.

A while ago, I had a conversation with a group of lay practitioners. They said, "Nowadays, even monastics may not have understood the Buddhadharma, let alone lay practitioners." I think they have a point. In our modern society, the majority believe that Buddhadharma is superstition or equate Buddhadharma to Qi Gong and heretics. Even those who have studied the Dharma believe that Dharma study is only for dispelling afflictive emotions and suffering; they are unaware of the truth of Buddhadharma—the teaching of non-arising.

Once a lay practitioner called and said, "Can I speak to Khenpo?"

Teasing him, I said, "He is not here in the ultimate meaning."

"Where is he?"

"He's been in the Palace of Dharmadhatu."

"What does he do there? When will he be back?"

"He works in a manner of being neither separate nor united. He might be back home when there is neither coming nor going."

Still not understanding, he said, "Could you please ask him to call me back when he gets home?"

As we see, some Buddha followers are quite unfamiliar with emptiness. I really wish that you gradually comprehend this principle: in the nature of reality, all phenomena are neither arising nor ceasing, neither coming nor going. If you could realize this, even if for one instant, it would transcend practicing approximate generosity.

What Is the Real Purpose of Accumulating Merit?

"Why? Because, Subhuti, bodhisattvas do not receive merit."

Subhuti asked the Buddha, "Bhagavan, what do you mean by 'bodhisattvas do not receive merit'?"

"Subhuti, bodhisattvas do not cling to the merit they have created, so it is said they do not receive merit."

The *Sixth Patriarch Platform Sutra* says, "Unknowing the genuine Dharma, (but) building monasteries for the sangha, practicing generosity, and setting up vegetarian feasts can only be called 'seeking merit.' Merit cannot become excellent qualities. Excellent qualities exist only in dharmakaya, not in accumulating merit."

In the conventional, accumulating merit brings the realization of the form body of the Buddha, and this causality is true and unerring; however, at the ultimate level, this is only mental fabrication, because bodhisattvas have no merit to attain. The *Heart Sutra* says, "Neither wisdom nor attainment."

What is the purpose of bodhisattvas' accumulating merit? It is to attain the state of not clinging to any characteristics, which is also the ultimate nature of phenomena. We should understand that to cling to Buddhadharma is also a form of cognitive obscuration, as there is neither the attainer nor the attained. The *Vimalakirti Sutra* says, "Ultimately, all phenomena do not exist." Since all phenomena do not exist, neither does merit. Merit is only an expedient phenomenon on the path of practice. When it is examined in the context of dharmakaya, bodhisattvas have no merit at all to attain.

In general, emptiness is the nature of reality of all phenomena. We should familiarize ourselves with this view regularly. If people who have not studied the Middle Way and the Great Perfection visualize that nothing exists only with their eyes closed, it is OK to start with this. However, as said in Mipham Rinpoche's *Beacon of Certainty*, this kind of practice is suitable only for beginners: though it can temporarily counteract attachment to true existence, it is not a practice that leads to ultimate reality.

29. Peaceful Deportment

Neither Coming nor Going Is the Reason for the Name "Tathagata"

"Subhuti, if somebody says the Tathagata comes and goes, sits and lies, this person must have not yet understood what I taught. Why? The Tathagata is called 'the Tathagata' for neither coming nor going."

Tathagata

TATHAGATA means "one who has thus come." Come to where? Come to the nature of all phenomena—reach the point where one can perceive things as they really are. There is great difference between the Tathagata and sentient beings. The latter cannot be called "Tathagata" because they have not yet dispelled delusive appearances and are still wandering in a samsara of endless birth and death.

Most people who have some knowledge of the history of Buddhism believe that the Tathagata must sometimes come and sometimes go, must sometimes sit down and sometimes lie down. Their reason is that initially, Buddha Shakyamuni descended to this human world from Tushita Heaven. After living here for eighty years—over the course of which he appeared in Deer Park, Vulture Peak Mountain, Shravasti, and other places—he entered parinirvana and went to the pure land. Even Basic Vehicle precepts frequently elaborate on the Buddha's daily deportment: how he walks, stands, sits, and lies down. Although we can accept these phenomena within the conventional, we cannot say this is the nature of reality. The Tathagata neither comes nor goes. As said in the sutra, "The nature of all phenomena is like the sky, neither abiding nor coming and going."

There is a story in the *Prajnaparamita Sutra* that relates to our discussion of buddhas' neither coming nor going. As Sadaprarudita looked everywhere for prajnaparamita teachings, one day he reached a broad field and saw that a tathagata appeared before him, instructed him how to find

Dharmodgota, and then completely disappeared. After going through incredible twists and turns and hardships, he finally saw Dharmodgota, and asked, "Where did the tathagata I've met come from and where did he go?" Upon hearing this question, Dharmodgota gave a teaching on the *Prajnaparamita Sutra* chapter "All Buddhas Neither Come nor Go," and then entered meditative concentration and remained in that state for seven years. This chapter uses lots of metaphors to explain the point that buddhas neither come nor go. For instance, just like a mirage: it comes from nowhere and goes nowhere, and such is the nature of all phenomena.

Likewise, the *Sutra Requested by the Old Lady* says, "All phenomena have never arisen, just like the sound of a drum." When a hand hits a drum, we hear the sound, but when we examine the origin of the sound, it comes neither from the drum nor the hand. We can see the analogy to neither coming nor going of all phenomena. And *The Fundamental Wisdom of the Middle Way* says, "Unceasing and unborn, neither nonexistent nor everlasting, neither several in meaning nor with a single meaning, neither coming nor going."

30. The Conception of Oneness

PARTICLES AS MANY AS DUST IN A SINGLE PARTICLE

"Subhuti, if a son or daughter of noble qualities crushes the three-thousandfold universe into particles, do you think the particles would be many?"

"A great many, Bhagavan. Why? If particles exist inherently, the Buddha would not say the particles would be many. Why? The Buddha said if the particles are a great many, it is because the particles do not exist, so it is said the particles are a great many."

IT IS NOT easy to comprehend the emptiness of particles because particles are minute. The intelligence and conceptual thoughts of human beings are limited, so we always perceive particles as truly existent. The Basic Vehicle believes that even at the ultimate level, the indivisible particles exist inherently, and many heretics also believe that particles last without changing. However, both the Middle Way school and the Hetuvidya school reject the notion that particles are permanent. *The Four Hundred Stanzas on the Middle Way* and *Guide to the Bodhisattva's Way of Life* offer great details refuting the wrong views of some Buddhist schools and of heretics. The *Avatamsaka Sutra* says, "There are particles as many as dust in one single particle," suggesting that particles do not truly exist.

When the Buddha said there are a great many particles, he meant at the conventional level. If we examine the question with the wisdom of noble beings entering the concentration of fundamental wisdom or with the wisdom free from mental fabrication, we understand that the essence of particles does not exist, so how can we say there are a great many particles?

The sutra says, "At the tip of a hair there are inconceivable fields in a variety of forms and shapes and completely distinct without mixing." If particles existed inherently, how could there be countless fields at the end of a hair? It is precisely because all phenomena are empty by nature that dependent origination can, inconceivably, appear in emptiness.

THIS WORLD IS NEITHER NONEXISTENT
NOR EVERLASTING

According to Buddhism, the smallest unit in the world is particles and the biggest unit in the world is the three-thousandfold universe. That particles do not truly exist has been explained; next is the nonexistence of the three-thousandfold universe:

"Bhagavan, the three-thousandfold universe taught by the Tathagata is not a universe, so it is called 'universe.'"

Sometimes Subhuti gave a great performance and sounded like he was teaching the Buddha. What he had said here could win him a perfect score.

At the ultimate level, up to Mount Meru and down to particles, there is no single phenomenon that exists inherently. In his *Introduction to the Middle Way*, Chandrakirti said, "Since the two truths are selfless by nature, they are neither nonexistent nor everlasting." Whether it is the material world or the sentient world, no phenomena have a self in nature at either the ultimate or conventional levels, so they are neither nonexistent nor everlasting. As a result, the Buddha teaches, "It is not universe, so it is called universe."

NOTHING IN THIS WORLD EXISTS INHERENTLY

"Why? If universe exists inherently, that is the conception of oneness."

The conception of oneness
The conception of oneness is an attachment toward the general form and characteristics of some entity. For instance, a vase is made up of particles, but we human beings always have a concept of oneness that allows us to call the aggregation of these particles a "vase."

Similarly, there is no "self" on top of the aggregation of the five aggregates—form (the physical world), sensation (our basic responses to experience), perception (interpretation of sense objects by mental labeling), mental formations (triggered by some object, which produce karma), and consciousness (including thoughts)—but because of this conception of oneness, we strongly attach a "self" to the combination of the five aggregates. In the same way, the material world consists of particles, but human beings view the gathering of all the insubstantial phenomena as a whole and treat it as truly existing. This is the conception of oneness.

"The Tathagata said oneness is not oneness, so it is called 'oneness.'"

As said in *The Four Hundred Stanzas on the Middle Way*, "Because of wrong attachment, people impute reality to aggregated phenomena." Things such as a vase, a car, a house, and so on, do not exist in themselves but are aggregates of various parts that people hold as familiar objects, label, and because of wrong attachment believe to truly exist. However, if examined with wisdom at the ultimate level, these objects are not real but are simply illusory reflections of onenesses. As said in *Guide to the Bodhisattva's Way of Life*, "[They are] unreal, like reflections in a mirror. How can you find anything real in [them]?"

Therefore the universe does not truly exist. As said in the *Perfect Enlightenment Sutra*, "Sentient beings and buddha fields are of the same nature as phenomena; hells and heavens are all pure lands." If we suppose the universe truly exists, then how can the buddha fields and the worlds of sentient beings be of the same nature? How can hells and heavens be pure lands? It is because the universe does not exist inherently, and because the nature of all phenomena is the same, that it can be stated in this way.

WORLDLY PEOPLE ARE PRONE TO MISTAKE "NONEXISTENCE" FOR "EXISTENCE"

"Subhuti, oneness is indescribable, but ordinary people attach to it."

The assertion of oneness in a vase, a pillar, and so forth is untenable not only in the Great Vehicle Middle Way school; even the Basic Vehicle *Abhidharma* concedes that oneness is an illusory phenomenon. Oneness does not exist inherently; it is free from mental fabrication. Unable to comprehend this principle, ordinary people often cling to the existence of oneness and fail to perceive the nature of ultimate reality.

For this reason, as recorded in many sutras, the Buddha said do not teach profound Dharma to ordinary beings because they are unable to take it in. The *Sutra of Elucidating the Profound Secret* says, "Being afraid that they would cling to a self, I do not present this topic to ignorant ordinary beings." The *Lotus Sutra* also says, "Since ordinary beings have superficial intelligence and strong attachment toward the five kinds of sensory desire, they could not understand the profound Dharma after hearing it, so it should not be taught to them."

Since the intelligence of ordinary people is so low, after hearing the Buddha's profound teachings, they are unable to understand the actual meaning and persist in the belief that phenomena exist inherently in the nature of reality. Ordinary people cannot comprehend the profound teachings because their capacities are limited and they have many causes for confusion: just as a person with eye disease always sees a hair in empty space, they cannot perceive the nature of ultimate reality of all phenomena.

For this reason, when Buddha Shakyamuni realized the perfect, unsurpassable enlightenment under the bodhi tree, he said, "The peaceful, profound, luminous, unconditioned Dharma free from mental fabrication—I have attained this sublime Dharma of ambrosia. Since anyone I teach would not understand it, I should quietly abide in the woods." After saying this, he did not teach any Dharma for forty-nine days. This is why he didn't turn the wheel of Dharma initially.

31. No Conception, No View

CLINGING TO SELF IS IMPURE, NOT CLINGING TO SELF IS PURE

"Subhuti, if someone says the Buddha said there are the conceptions of a self, a person, a sentient being, and a living being, Subhuti, what do you think? Does this person understand what I have said?"

"No, Bhagavan, this person does not understand what you have said. Why? Because the Tathagata said the conceptions of a self, a person, a sentient being, and a living being are not the conceptions of a self, a person, a sentient being, and a living being, so they are called 'the conceptions of a self, a person, a sentient being, and a living being.'"

WHY DID the Buddha ask this question? He asked it because in order to "tame" sentient beings of different capacities, he gave a variety of teachings. Knowing the capacity of beginners, he gave them a version of the teachings based on an existing self.

The *Agama Sutra* and *Vinaya Sutra* of the Basic Vehicle say, "I exist in the nature of reality." In a number of the Buddha's stories, he refers to "my retinue" and "my sponsors," and he says, "at the causal stage, I was reborn as . . ." He also sometimes says, "I had a headache," and "once in a past life, I was born as a son of a fisherman." Therefore it seems that in some scriptures Buddha Shakyamuni had the conceptions of a self, a person, a sentient being, and a living being. Seeing this, some people believe it is tenable to say these conceptions exist inherently.

But is this the ultimate view of the Buddha? Subhuti said no, and if anyone thinks so, they have not yet understood the intended meaning of the Buddha. For instance, the *Tathagatagarbha Sutra* says that although it was said that "I" is permanent and the buddha nature of sentient beings is changeless, this was stated from the perspective of the luminous aspect of the third turning of the wheel of Dharma. When speaking from the emptiness aspect of the second turning of the wheel of Dharma, "I" and "buddha nature" do not exist intrinsically. As said in the *Vimalakirti Sutra*, "Clinging to self is impure, not clinging to self is pure."

The Sixth Patriarch explained the four conceptions in the following way:

The conception of a self: Taking the essence of the Tathagatagarbha as inherently existent.

The conception of a person: Taking the uncontaminated nature of sentient being as inherently existent.

The conception of a sentient being: The afflictive emotions of sentient beings are primordially pure, so taking this pure attribute as inherently existent.

The conception of a living being: In the nature of ultimate reality, all sentient beings are unborn and unceasing, so taking the attribute of unborn and unceasing as inherently existent.

The Sixth Patriarch articulated it concisely, but the meaning is profound and thoroughly vast. Once you grasp this, you will be able to understand why the Buddha said the conception of a self, a person, a sentient being, and a living being is precisely not the conception of a self, a person, a sentient being, and a living being.

The essence of all the teachings of the Buddha can be summarized in the emptiness of selflessness, which, when realized, is capable of destroying any wrong views. As *The Four Hundred Stanzas on the Middle Way* says, "The wonderful principle of emptiness, of selflessness, is the genuine state of all the buddhas—it can destroy all vicious views and can bring nirvana; it is the nondual teaching."

The four conceptions do not exist, so why did the Buddha talk about them? In *The Introduction to the Middle Way*, Chandrakirti explained it well: "Just as the Buddha who transcends *satkāya-drsti* (the view of self) still talks about 'I' and 'mine,' phenomena do not exist inherently in nature but sutras with practical meaning still claim they truly exist." The Buddha had long ago transcended the view of self, but he appeared to talk about the self and what belongs to the self often; similarly, although all phenomena have no inherent existence, in sutras not presenting the definitive meaning, the Buddha also said that the independent nature of phenomena exists and that "I" exists.

In general, the four conceptions exist within the conventional but do not exist at the ultimate level. Here the sutra examines the selflessness of people and the selflessness of phenomena from the standpoint of view (before practice, conduct, or fruition). It is very important to develop the right view in one's mind.

LISTEN FIRST AND THEN REFLECT, AND LAST, MEDITATE

Next is the conclusion.

"Subhuti, those who have generated the perfect, unsurpassable bodhichitta should understand, perceive, and believe all phenomena in this way and avoid giving rise to characteristics."

The theme of this sutra is to dispel the attachment to characteristics, so some Chan masters call the *Diamond Cutter Sutra* the *Commentary Dispelling Characteristics.* This passage of the *Diamond Cutter Sutra* is the most profound: just as a teacher directly pointing out the nature of mind for the disciple in the tradition of the Great Perfection!

After studying this supreme Dharma of the Great Vehicle, we should do our best to absorb the Dharma into our mind and gain some understanding of the nature of phenomena, persistently inquiring, What is the nature of ultimate reality of all phenomena? What is no form or characteristics? and so on.

No matter what kind of Dharma we study, we should feel like we are drinking ambrosia. Without thoroughly assimilating the teachings, no matter how many of them we have heard, they won't have a positive effect when we encounter afflictive emotions and unfavorable conditions.

Understand
Understand refers to the wisdom arising from listening. After generating bodhichitta, one should first listen to the Dharma before a qualified teacher in an appropriate manner.

Perceive
Perceive refers to the wisdom arising from reflecting. After hearing the teaching, one should repeatedly reflect on the meaning and realize the nature of all phenomena.

Believe

Believe refers to the wisdom arising from meditating. Since what has been realized through reflection can easily be forgotten, we need to meditate on it again and again. In this way, we are able to attain irreversible certainty on the realization.

First understand, then realize, and finally, gain certainty. By listening, reflecting, and meditating, we can achieve the spontaneous arising of the emptiness of prajna that is distinctive, empty, and yet appearing.

The connotations of this sutra passage are so profound that a Chan master reached enlightenment relying on it.

In the past, Chan Master Da Yu Shou Zhi had a disciple who diligently chanted the *Diamond Cutter Sutra* a hundred times every day. One day, the master asked the disciple, "You chant the *Diamond Cutter Sutra* so many times every day, what on earth does it say?" The disciple could not say even one word in response. The Master said, "Why don't you chant less but spend some time contemplating the meaning?" The disciple followed the master's instruction, chanting the sutra once daily, doing his best to understand the meaning, until one day, while chanting "should understand, perceive, and believe it in this way," he suddenly awakened.

The Characteristics of No Characteristics Is the Genuine Ultimate Reality

"Subhuti, the so-called characteristics as said by the Tathagata are not characteristics but only called 'characteristics.'"

The Buddha talked about six characteristics in the *Avatamsaka Sutra*, three characteristics in the *Sutra Revealing the Profound Meaning*, four characteristics in the *Diamond Cutter Sutra*, and three characteristics in *The Great Treatise on the Perfection of Wisdom*. All of these characteristics do not exist at the ultimate level; they are all illusory. The characteristics of no characteristics is the genuine ultimate reality.

The *Sixth Patriarch Platform Sutra* also says, "No characteristics is the essence." Without transcending characteristics we can realize neither the selflessness of people and phenomena nor the primordial wisdom.

32. What Appears Is Not Real

THE THREE GREATEST MERITS IN THE WORLD

THIS LAST CHAPTER summarizes the merit of the *Diamond Cutter Sutra*.

"Subhuti, if someone gives away seven jewels that fill up countless universes, and if a son or daughter of noble qualities generates bodhichitta, upholds, recites, and teaches this sutra or even a four-line verse of it to others, the merit of the latter excels that of the former."

Generate bodhichitta
When we chant the *Diamond Cutter Sutra*, it is better to start with taking refuge and generating bodhichitta and finish with dedication. If virtuous actions are imbued with the three supremenesses,[11] no matter what virtuous actions we engage in, the merit would be much greater.

Teach
Teach the *Diamond Cutter Sutra* often, whenever you have a chance to teach the Dharma. If circumstances do not allow you to teach the entire sutra, focus on the following verse: *All conditioned phenomena are like dreams, illusions, water bubbles, reflections, dew, lightning.* It won't take much time, and with a pure motivation, the merit would be immense. It is the best way to accumulate merit.

Why is it of immense merit? Because chanting, upholding, and teaching sutras belong to the ten Dharma conducts. Since this sutra mainly explains the emptiness of prajna, which is the origin of all the buddhas, the merit would be inconceivable.

In *The Gateway to Knowledge*, Mipham Rinpoche said, "There are three things that are of the greatest merit in this world: first, generating bodhichitta; second, teaching the Dharma of the Great Vehicle; and third, meditating on emptiness." Since this sutra is about emptiness, we should always listen, reflect, and meditate on it, and at least chant this sutra once every day.

A great master also said, "Since we have obtained human bodies in this life, if we are incapable of listening, reflecting, or meditating, we should at least chant some Vajra words with the blessing of the lineage masters every day. In this way we can attain supreme merit."

Some people believe that it is of great merit to offer their teacher $100 and a khata,[12] and that it does not matter whether they chant the *Diamond Cutter Sutra* or not. This means they do not understand the meaning of this sutra. Practicing generosity can create merit, this is undoubtedly so, yet what brings the greatest merit? Meditating on emptiness, generating bodhichitta, and teaching the Dharma of the Great Vehicle!

THE STATE OF "MEDITATIVE CONCENTRATION" TRANSCENDS ANY CHARACTERISTIC

All the eighty-four-thousand teachings of Buddha Shakyamuni are aimed to guide sentient beings to realize the emptiness of prajna and enter the ultimate nature of all phenomena. What is the ultimate nature of all phenomena? It can be realized in meditative concentration and the post-meditation state.

"How to teach others? Without grasping at any characteristic, just keep (your mind) motionless."

This is the root of all meditative concentration: the mind does not grasp any characteristic, is free from mental fabrication, abides in emptiness without movement, and does not give rise to the slightest conceptual thought, just like the empty sky.

If such a state is able to arise, it surpasses the merit of any kind of virtuous action, including generating bodhichitta. Just as said in the *All Phenomena Are Inconceivable Sutra*, "The merit of upholding the sublime Dharma and generating bodhichitta is not even one-sixteenth as great as the merit of meditating on emptiness." *The Mind Mirror Collection* also says, "If someone upholds the sublime Dharma and generates bodhichitta, it cannot match even one-sixteenth of the merit of meditating on emptiness."

Therefore, it is of inconceivable merit to teach others emptiness and make them abide in this state for a very short time!

IN "POST MEDITATION" EVERYTHING IS SEEN LIKE DREAMS AND ILLUSIONS

"Why? All conditioned phenomena are like dreams, illusions, water bubbles, reflections, dew, lightning. Visualize in this way."

In the post-meditation state, we should view all phenomena as dreams and illusions because they are all conditioned phenomena arising from causes and conditions and are not truly existent. There are six similes to illustrate this theory:

Dreams: Dreams arise from confused consciousness. In a dream the dualistic objects and subjects seem to exist but in fact have not the slightest essence.

Illusions: Illusions are created by magicians with tricks; they do not inherently exist.

Water bubbles: Water bubbles arise from causes and conditions but disappear momentarily.

Reflections: Reflections appear only when causes and conditions are present; they appear vividly but are empty by nature.

Dew: Dew swiftly vanishes when the sun rises.

Lightning: Lightning appears in the present instant but ceases in the next.

These six similes illustrate the nature of all phenomena in their two aspects: empty in nature and impermanent. In the Tibetan edition, these similes are followed by another four: meteors, eye disease, lamp, and clouds, for a total of ten similes. These ten are also in the translation by Xuan Zang. Kumarajiva's version has only six similes (perhaps because he used a different Sanskrit version or the other four were omitted during the translation). However, since the meaning is not too different and Kumarajiva's true words are of great blessing, there is no need to adjust the text here.

The *Diamond Cutter Sutra* has six or ten similes for conditioned phenomena that do not exist. Other Buddhist sutras usually employ eight similes of illusion. In the *Liberation through Hearing Sutra* there are twelve similes on illusion.

The *Sutra Requested by Subahu* says, "All things of the three times are like illusions." The *Agama Sutra* says, "Form is like aggregated foam, feeling is like floating water bubbles, perception is like wild horses, mental formation is like plantain trees, and consciousness is like illusions." The *Fundamental Wisdom of the Middle Way* says, "Like illusions, like dreams, like the city of gandhavas, whatever arises, abides, and ceases is just like this."

In a word, there are numerous scriptural authorities like these, which draw on similes to teach that all phenomena are empty and impermanent in nature.

The Virtuous Ending—The Conclusion

With Joy Everyone Gains Faith and Follows the Instruction

After the Buddha finished this sutra, Venerable Subhuti, all the monks, nuns, male and female lay practitioners, as well as gods, humans, and asuras in this world were delighted by and gained faith in what the Buddha taught and applied it in practice.

While teaching this sutra, no unfavorable conditions appeared, and today we have finished it perfectly!

After hearing this teaching, many people must be extremely happy and eager to praise the merit of Buddha Shakyamuni.

Let us dedicate the merit of this virtue to all sentient beings. May all sentient beings be free from suffering, attain happiness, and soon reach enlightenment! We also dedicate this virtue for world peace and good weather! And may the six sessions of every single day be auspicious!

Postscript

MAY MORE PEOPLE FURTHER THEIR UNDERSTANDING OF THE *DIAMOND CUTTER SUTRA*

WHILE STUDYING the *Diamond Cutter Sutra*, you might notice unfamiliar Buddhist terminology, such as "the two truths," or "definitive meaning." Since the sutra's meaning is profound, it is necessary to use such terms to explain the text clearly. If you wish to gain a more thorough understanding of these terms, you can study other texts on the Middle Way, such as *The Fundamental Wisdom of the Middle Way*, *The Introduction to the Middle Way*, *The Four Hundred Stanzas on the Middle Way*, and so forth, which are all available in reliable English translations.

The fact is, if you wish to realize the emptiness of prajna, or transcendental wisdom, you must make a great effort. Attaining realization requires long study and practice. Just reading a book won't take you to that goal.

It is worth mentioning that in teaching this sutra, I have, according to the Tibetan Buddhist tradition, quoted the instructions of a number of buddhas, bodhisattvas, and past noble beings in order to support the ideas presented here. If one followed only one's own conceptual thoughts and taught whatever one liked, it would be hard to tell if what one taught is correct or wrong, medicine or poison, for sentient beings.

However, my intelligence is limited, so what I have explained is not perfect. Yet I wish my commonplace remarks could inspire others to come up with more valuable commentaries, and I wish more people could further their understanding of the *Diamond Cutter Sutra*. If you benefited by just one line of this book, I would be greatly gratified!

Sodargye
Larung Gar, Sertar

Notes

1. *Prajna* is a Sanskrit word commonly translated as "transcendental wisdom." In the mundane sense, *prajna* represents a sharpening of perception and inquiry into the true nature of reality—that is, impermanence, dissatisfaction, non-self, and emptiness. Prajna is the means by which we perceive emptiness: it is a state of pure consciousness that transcends worldly concepts or beliefs that impede perfect wisdom. It is considered to be direct insight into the truth received from the teachings of Buddha and it is needed to reach enlightenment.

2. Different Sanskrit versions are not uncommon. *Guide to the Bodhisattva's Way of Life* fell prey to a dispute over how many verses it really contained even at the time of Shantideva (685–783). Panditas from Kashmir said there were over one thousand verses, panditas from eastern India insisted there must be seven hundred verses, while panditas from central India claimed there were exactly one thousand verses. Finally, the author, the bodhisattva Shantideva, confirmed that one thousand verses was correct.

3. Referring to the doctrine of emptiness here.

4. In Chinese, the terms "characteristic" and "conception" have the same pronunciation but different tones, the former the fourth tone and the latter the third. However, the structure of these two characters differs by only one component: mind. If "characteristic" is put on top of the character "mind," the word becomes "conception." Meaning that when the mind grasps "characteristic" it is "conception." So in this sutra, although only the term "characteristic" is used when referring to these four characteristics (相), the meaning is sometimes "the four conceptions" (想). Earlier, in chapter 3, "The Genuine Great Vehicle," we saw that Xuan Zang translated this as "perception," so that "characteristic" and "perception" have the same meaning.

5. According to the *Abhidharmakosha*, Mount Meru is as high as 160,000 yojanas, which is equal to 1,068,800 kilometers. The body of Rahu, the king of the asuras, was said to be exactly as huge as Mount Meru.

6. The "thirty-two major excellent marks" of the Buddha have been expounded in *The Great Treatise on the Perfection of Wisdom*, *The Ornament of Clear Realization*, and *The Precious Garland of the Middle Way*. The "ten powers" have been explained in *The Introduction to the Middle Way*. "The eighteen extraordinary attributes" have been elaborated in *The Gateway to Knowledge* by Mipham Rinpoche.

7. Through the accumulation of merit over countless eons, the Buddha developed supreme marks on his body, such as the ushnisha on the crown of his head and the white hair between his eyebrows. There is no single ugly mark on the entire body of the Buddha.

8. This period of time is the cause of his enlightenment, hence it is called his "causal stage" (因地), literally the time before the Buddha became the Buddha.

9. Real functioning phenomena are things that have a function, like a table or a computer, whereas unreal phenomena do not have a function, like empty space (although one might argue that empty space has the function of holding everything, when all phenomena are categorized, empty space is said to be an unreal phenomenon).

10. "Mind" is pronounced the same as "sum." "Dim" has the same sound as "pointing." The granny asked him rather ingenuously, "Which pastry do you want?" In the content of the *Diamond Cutter Sutra*, her meaning is, "Which mind do you point to among the three minds of the three times?"

11. The supremeness of beginning is generating bodhichitta, the supremeness of actual action is fixating on no objects, and the supremeness of conclusion is dedication.

12. A khata is a traditional ceremonial scarf in Tibetan Buddhism. It is the custom to bring a khata when visiting a temple, shrine, or teacher as a way of showing gratitude for the kindness of your teacher.

Index

About the Author

KHENPO SODARGYE was born in Tibet in 1962 in what is today the Sichuan Province of China. He spent his early years herding yaks, and after attending Garze Normal School entered Larung Gar Buddhist Institute in Sertar, becoming a monk in 1985 under the great Jigme Phuntsok Rinpoche. Khenpo served Rinpoche as his personal and teaching interpreter on overseas tours in Asia, Europe, and North America as well as at Larung Gar. Khenpo has taught and translated the Dharma for over thirty years and has lectured on Buddhism and social issues in over a hundred universities around the world. He is one of the leading scholars at Larung Gar and has popularized Tibetan Buddhism among Han Chinese students with numerous bestselling books.

What to Read Next from Wisdom Publications

Tales for Transforming Adversity
A Buddhist Lama's Advice for Life's Ups and Downs
Khenpo Sodargye

Enjoy a variety of meditations on topics from flattery and jealousy to karma and compassion. In each brief chapter Khenpo Sodargye weaves in stories from ancient classics and modern headlines.

What Makes You So Busy?
Finding Peace in the Modern World
Khenpo Sodargye

"*What Makes You So Busy?* is a wonderfully down-to-earth, practical volume of wise counsel. Khenpo Sodargye shows the way to find happiness and contentment whether one is a monastic leading a life of seclusion or a layperson immersed in a socially active way of life. In doing so, he has done us all a great service."—B. Alan Wallace, president, Santa Barbara Institute for Consciousness Studies

Always Remembering
Heartfelt Advice for Your Entire Life
His Holiness Jigme Phuntsok
Translated by Khenpo Sodargye

In memory of the thirteenth anniversary of Rinpoche's passing, this memorial book was compiled based on audio recordings of his precious and renowned teachings.

The Diamond Sutra
Transforming the Way We Perceive the World
Mu Soeng

"A fresh and inspiring exposition of core Mahayana philosophy. Mu Soeng's commentary on *The Diamond Sutra* is a combination Buddhist history lesson, philosophical investigation, and thorough contemporary reading of this core Mahayana text."—*Inquiring Mind*

Describing the Indescribable
A Commentary on the Diamond Sutra
Master Hsing Yun
Translated by Tom Graham

"A brilliant translation with a lucid and accessible commentary. Master Hsing Yun is truly a leading light of contemporary Chinese Buddhism."
—Professor Lance E. Nelson, University of San Diego

Fathoming the Mind
Inquiry and Insight in Düdjom Lingpa's Vajra Essence
B. Alan Wallace

Fathoming the Mind continues the commentary to Düdjom Lingpa's *Vajra Essence* that appeared in *Stilling the Mind*, daringly contextualizing Buddhist teachings on the Great Perfection as a revolutionary challenge to many contemporary beliefs. This companion volume stems from an oral commentary that B. Alan Wallace gave to the next section of the *Vajra Essence*, on the cultivation of contemplative insight, or vipaśyanā, that fathoms the nature of existence as a whole.

The Path
A Guide to Happiness
Khenpo Sherab Zangpo

The Path brings us the remarkable teachings of Khenpo Sherab Zangpo, a leading scholar from the famous Larung Buddhist Institute of Five Sciences in Eastern Tibet. As a lineage holder in the tradition of the Great Perfection—the highest teachings of the Nyingma school of Tibetan Buddhism—Khenpo Sherab offers insight into the nature of our world and the possibility of transformation through committed engagement with the path.

The Rice Seedling Sutra
Buddha's Teachings on Dependent Arising
Geshe Yeshe Thabkhe

"Dependent arising, one of the Buddha's most profound teachings, is brought to life in this lucid commentary on the *Rice Seedling Sutra* by Geshe Yeshe Thabkhe, one of the greatest living scholars of the Tibetan tradition."—José Ignacio Cabezón, Dalai Lama Professor of Tibetan Buddhism and Cultural Studies, UC Santa Barbara

Nāgārjuna's Wisdom
A Practitioner's Guide to the Middle Way
Barry Kerzin

"Venerable Barry Kerzin offers a remarkable guide to the key insights and reasoning that are at the heart of Nāgārjuna's famed Middle Way philosophy. Thanks to this book any serious Buddhist practitioner can now appreciate why the Tibetan tradition makes so much fuss about Nāgārjuna and his wisdom."—Thupten Jinpa, principal English translator to His Holiness the Dalai Lama and author of *Self, Reality, and Reason in Tibetan Philosophy*

About Wisdom Publications

Wisdom Publications is the leading publisher of classic and contemporary Buddhist books and practical works on mindfulness. To learn more about us or to explore our other books, please visit our website at wisdomexperience.org or contact us at the address below.

Wisdom Publications
199 Elm Street
Somerville, MA 02144 USA

We are a 501(c)(3) organization, and donations in support of our mission are tax deductible.

Wisdom Publications is affiliated with the Foundation for the Preservation of the Mahayana Tradition (FPMT).